N

THE ART OF STRATEGICALLY POSSESSING YOUR POSSESSION

Proven Biblical Principles and Strategies to Launch You Into Your Purpose

Tracey-Ann Wright

ISBN: 978-1-953759-61-0 (paperback)

Printed in the United States of America

Scripture quotations marked (NIV) are taken from the Holy Bible, New International Version®, NIV®. Copyright © 1973, 1978, 1984 by Biblica, Inc.™ Used by permission of Zondervan. All rights reserved worldwide.

Scripture quotations marked "KJV" are taken from the Holy Bible, King James Version (Public Domain).

Scripture quotations marked (NLT) are taken from the Holy Bible, New Living Translation, copyright © 1996, 2004, 2007 by Tyndale House Foundation. Used by permission of Tyndale House Publishers, Inc., Carol Stream, Illinois 60188. All rights reserved.

Scripture quotations marked "NKJV" are taken from the New King James Version. Copyright © 1982 by Thomas Nelson, Inc.

DEDICATION

I dedicate this book to the people in my life who have been there with me through the valley moments when it seems like possessing God's promises was an illusion.

To my mother, Pauline Cole, who taught me that God's plans for me is to have a bright future and an expected end. Thank you, mommy, for your sacrifice, care and guidance. Thank you for being there to take care of my children when I had to travel to meetings and when I was too focused on writing and developing the other project that God had rested on my heart.

To my children, Jonelle, Jadalaa, and Jahi, you are my joy and source of inspiration. Jonelle, your level of maturity and wisdom is admirable and sometimes unfathomable. Thank you for your thought-provoking questions that have influenced the content. To my boys, thank you for showering me with kind words on a daily basis of how wonderful and beautiful I am to you. The experience of seeing you all grow from beautiful babies into respectful children is a source of wisdom, inspiration, and strength.

ACKNOWLEDGMENTS

The writing of this book could not have been possible without the guidance of the Holy Spirit who is the Director of my life.

I would also like to thank those individuals who have been aligned with me to make the manifestation of this book a reality. First, for those directly involved: my family and close friends, Marsha, Colleen, Stephanie, I could not have done this without your support and kind words of encouragement.

I want to thank my warrior partners (my spiritual support system) who have been there for the early morning prayer meetings and the late-night prayer calls from which this book was birthed.

Thanks to Prophetess Hope McDowell-Gibson, my mother in the prophetic. Thank you for being the voice of the Holy Spirit and speaking into my life those things which I can see manifesting today. Thank you for your guidance and birthing instructions on how to wage the good warfare over our prophetic words.

Thanks to Pastor Alfred Rampersaud and Lady Linda. Thank you for the teachings and for being the listening ears during my brainstorming process.

I offer sincere thanks to the entire Living Faith Community Church of God in Calgary. Thanks for the encouragement and support.

Thanks to my business associates to whom I am indebted. I thank you for the listening ear as well as for being my accountability partners on this journey. Thanks to the Unmask Your Beauty team in Calgary for holding me accountable and being there when I needed information that was necessary to make the publication a reality.

Thanks to the Lord God, who gives me strength, wisdom and creative blessings.

FOREWORD

MASTERING THE ART OF STRATEGICALLY POSSESSING YOUR POSSESSION is a must-read book. It is undoubtedly for the reader seeking to understand their purpose and fulfill their God-given mandate in the earth.

In her own unique style, Tracey-Ann fuses together a compendium of strategies to create a road map on how to strategically possess all the riches God has deposited in Jesus Christ for us.

The book is well balanced and is in an easy-to-read format. Get ready to be captivated and mesmerized!

With her strong professional background and spiritual depth, Tracey-Ann has skillfully managed to knit corporate tools and strategies with biblical principles to form a most lethal rocket to success. You will surely be on your way to great conquest.

You will be inspired and blessed by her practical insights and personal testimonies that have paved her journey. You will be challenged as you learn how to be laser-focus on the route to possess your possession. You will appreciate her reasoning behind the need to follow your plan A and realizing the need for godly counsel. Scattered with techniques, you will discover the benefits of strategic partnership and also the knowledge of when to go alone.

Packed with encouragement and motivation, this book assures you that failure is not final. It is a work of hope intentionally designed to spur you to tap into the unlimited power of an Omnipotent God.

I was rather impressed with the planning and analytical tools that she shared, utilizing biblical references and enabling them to come alive and be easily understood.

Tracey-Ann manages to beautifully chronicle a list of power moves that will serve as catalysts for the believer to possess their possession.

With the use of various literary devices, you can't help but enjoy the delectable way she pens the way forward for the believer to walk in strength and power.

This work of art is from a serial winner and has harnessed the insights of many notable scholars who have helped to impact our world.

You will be excited that you have obtained this value for money tool kit that will be a quintessential aid in mastering the art of strategically possessing your possession.

Demoy Nash
J.P., MA, B-Tech, ASc., Dip.

FOREWORD

Tracey-Ann and I met on the first day of first form and immediately became so close we declared ourselves best friends within days. I look back on those times fondly thinking of the perfect lives we planned to lead and how certain we were that success was guaranteed. Our world seemed limitless, our outlook certain, and our actions dictated immediate results. But then we grew up, graduated high school, went to college. Our life and career paths diverged, but we would reconnect 3 or 4 times a year for birthdays, holidays, big life events, sometimes only by phone, but each experience was always immensely pleasurable in the way only time with an old best friend can be.

Sometime in around 2009, during a particularly devastating period for both of us, one us asked the other what happened to us? How is it that life never delivered what it promised? Certainly we deserved it. We were educated, intelligent, beautiful, hardworking, eager to learn and to please, so why was it taking so long for all our dreams to come to fruition? How had the perfectly planned future we expected to just walk into somehow been so elusive? Why were we being passed over? Our conversations were now almost daily as we explored these topics in depth. We needed different men to date, we needed to develop an entrepreneurial spirit, we needed a plan, we needed a vision board, we each needed to write a book, we needed to rethink our approach, we needed more degrees, we needed to clear our minds, we needed to open them, maybe we needed Jesus! At the time I laughed it off, but it was around that time that Tracey started taking her relationship with God more seriously. Over time, I noticed the subtle change in her language. *God did it; Jesus blocked it. God opened that one door. The Holy Spirit told me not to.* I had to ask: "Are you born again?"

"No, I'm not born again," she said, "But I'm trying to incorporate God more into my life and my decisions."

A couple of years pass, and her Bible studying showed. Her speech was riddled with Bible verses verbatim. More time passed and she announced she was saved. In no time she was a youth leader in church. I received a video clip of her preaching, yes, preaching—anointed, Holy Ghost touched. I was so happy watching her. I could clearly see that she was truly where she was meant to be.

Suddenly, our conversation was elevated; our analysis was no longer aimless but was framed by God's promises. We never kept our side; we lived in doubt and lacked faith; the weaknesses we succumbed to instead of relying on God's strength. She led me to understand why we kept failing because we were not building on the Lord; we were financially bereft because we were not tithing. She grew more discerning, and I saw real changes in her life. I saw her rise above insurmountable challenges, walked away from situations that kept her trapped, and watched her shed false friends and alliances. She grew more measured, calmer, her wisdom was deeper, and then she started to build her house, her new life plan, and build up her family again. To witness this was in itself a miracle, but I was more than a witness; I was a part of it. I was applying her approach to my own life and sharing it with other friends who were themselves searching.

Sometime last year (2020), Tracey talked about her calling to write this book, but admitted she was still praying about how to compile the contents of her journals. I imagined it would be an autobiographical account of some kind as one of her favorite sayings is "My life is a testimony." And then I read it. I was overwhelmed on so many levels. I was overjoyed with what she had produced but also immensely saddened and wistful.

How much better would our lives had been if we had followed the path laid out for us in the book? How many pitfalls would have been avoided? While we tried to fix our lives on our own and racked or brains for answers and fixes, we kept drawing blanks because we had not been attuned to listen to the Holy Spirit. We were not studying the Scriptures to find the answers. We were not praying meaningfully to be in communion with God, but we were telling Him what we wanted to happen and when. Access to this knowledge would have redirected our efforts. Our labors would not have been in vain.

Every stage in life when you are faced with big decisions, any day that seemed particularly challenging, any time you are at risk of being overwhelmed, this book will guide you to a resolution where God and His promises are at the foundation. If you want to remove doubt and indecision, this book will show you how to have the faith you need. For the trauma and suffering you endured, it shows you how to claim your deliverance.

This book serves as an essential toolbox to build a master plan, remain true to it and achieve the goals God laid out for you. When you are vulnerable to being sidetracked from that plan, even then God will ensure victory because the path you walk is protected. You will watch limits melt away, hesitancy will float into the past, and you will rejoice in living the life you always knew you were meant to lead.

Marsha Mighty
Chemist, Quality Manager

FOREWORD

*T*he Art of Strategic Possession – Mastering the Art of Strategically Possessing Your Possession* is a revelatory treasure box for anyone who desires to discover the essence of their existence and succeed at it.

Are you searching for the secret to excelling in every area of your life with ease? Then, I am delighted to announce to you that your search is over!

Perhaps you are familiar with the Biblical phrase "Possess your possession" in Obadiah 1:17, or you might think that all you need to possess your possession are several rounds of fervent prayers and warfare encounters. As such, you may want to pass over this book; please don't. There is always something new to learn, no matter how familiar the topic might be. Thankfully, I kept an open mind. As a result, I discovered that this book is more than a reminder to pray more, but a contemporary, practical, and relatable guide to taking hold of all of life's goodness.

I also enjoyed how Tracey utilized some insights from her professional experience to explain some points further. It goes to emphasize that everything in our life is valuable to God.

I had a lot to take away from this book, but one that will stay with me forever is the lesson to eliminate my plan Bs. I will also ensure to put to use those helpful tips Tracey shared about protecting visions.

No doubt, *The Art of Strategic Possession – Mastering the Art of Strategically Possessing Your Possession* is an astonishing piece of knowledge, the type you will have to keep referring back to.

What Tracey has done here in this book is profound, and I am in awe of her personality so much more now than when I first encountered her through the Unmask Your Beauty platform.

Tracey exudes such confidence, warmth, and calm simultaneously, always beaming with smiles, like she has no single worry in the world. Now I know why; her secrets are all out here in this book.

This book also confirms that Tracey is undoubtedly a generous giver because she has painstakingly documented her revelations and experiences with its expository writing style. How gracious of her to desire that every person experience this same light. The fantastic thing about this type of light is that its illumination is different for each person, so get ready to have your unique experience and revelations too.

There is a *"what"* to succeed in life. This book will expose you to the *"how"* you will possess all life has in stock for you. Therefore, I invite you to begin this journey of discovering the art of strategic possession so you can start to master this art of possessing your (kingdom) possessions such as salvation, healing, wisdom, wealth, consistent success at all endeavours, marital bliss, peaceful mind, exceptional children, and so much more, that was specially set aside for just you.

Wow! I am excited for you already!

Jolade Osuntubo
The Visions Midwife

TABLE OF CONTENTS

INTRODUCTION

The lines have fallen for me in pleasant places; surely I have a delightful inheritance. I will praise the LORD, who counsels me; even at night my heart instructs me. I have set the LORD always before me. Because he is at my right hand, I will not be shaken. (Psalm 16:6-8 – NIV)

Did you know you were born for greatness? Yes, my friend! You were born to take dominion and dominate in the earth realm. In this book, I will share biblical principles for taking possession and dominating in your sphere of influence, whether it be in your personal, family, career or community life. You will become clear on each phase for possessing your possession and will be equipped with strategies to help you maintain.

But first, let me clarify the meaning of the famous quote "Possess your Possession." I believe this is one of the most quoted phrases from the Bible, and to some, it is a cliché. However, when the Holy Spirit opened my eyes to it, I realized there was much depth to this famous phrase than what many understood it to be.

Every child of God has an inheritance in Christ. Through Jesus Christ, the believer has become an

28

heir of God and a joint-heir with Jesus Christ. Because of this fact, salvation, healing, good health, deliverance, peace, happiness, divine protection, guidance, prosperity, and success is their divine birthright. It is the same for you reading this book today. In a nutshell, this is your possession, and it is this inheritance that we are to take possession of. We must walk in authority and dominion to achieve our God-given purpose.

The first key to possess your possession is to take practical steps to claim those things God says belong to you, whether it is kingdoms (financial, educational, governmental, entertainment), territories, or land. Many individuals often make the mistake of thinking that their possessions will come to them on a platter or drop from the sky with no effort on their part. If you are familiar with the Bible, you will remember that at the time God gave the Promised Land to the children of Israel, it was not a vacant land; to the contrary, the land was fully occupied by the Canaanites, Hittites, Amorites, Perizzites, Jebusites, and the Girgashites who were the original owners and occupiers. You will come to realize that behind every command of God, there is the omnipotent power of God to carry out that command. Once you accept that it is not by might or

29

by power but by the Spirit of the Lord, you will begin to walk in your possession.

It might seem easy to say; however, it takes a great deal of faith to walk in your purpose and calling. Faith is having the firm belief that the thing you hoped for, that which you have yet to see in your physical reality, will come to pass. It is the confidence that your dreams and visions will materialize in the natural, regardless of your present circumstance.

To manifest your vision, it is important that you gain an understanding of the keys, principles, and strategies required. One such strategy is the law of possession. The Lord had given all the land to the children of Israel, but the law of possession needed to be activated. The activation was that "every square meter of the land of Canaan you set your foot upon, that is what I have given to you—no more and no less." This is how it is with our physical blessings as well as our spiritual blessings. There are many blessings that are available to us today. Just as God gave the land to the children of Israel, God gives all blessings to every believer; some believers possess those spiritual blessings, and some do not. You may ask yourself, why is this so? The key is very practical. You must set your foot upon them; you have to occupy and dominate and take possession. I will share with you the blueprint to activate the law of possessing your possession so you may experience your heaven on earth.

PHASE 1:

THE ALIGNMENT/QUICKENING

For all who are led by the Spirit of God are sons of God. For you did not receive the spirit of slavery to fall back into fear, but you have received the Spirit of adoption as sons, by whom we cry, "Abba! Father!" The Spirit himself bears witness with our spirit that we are children of God. (Romans 8:14–16 - ESV).

With every great manifestation, there needs to be a quickening or the coming to life of that dream, vision or desire that has been lying dormant on the inside of you. This is what I coined to be the "aha" moment or the great realization that you are indeed a child of the most high God, and you have an abundant life waiting for you to manifest.

Every child of God has an inheritance in Christ. Even though many are born again, many fail to come into the realization of who they truly are and how to step into that purpose of living the will of God. This time can be really painful, and though God has given us all we need, we can remain stuck. This reminds me of the story of the chained elephant. This gigantic elephant was being held by only a small rope tied to its front leg. No chains, no cages. One would think that the elephant was powerful enough to break away from the bonds at any time, but for some reason, it did not. Investigations revealed that when the elephant was very young and much smaller, the same size rope was used to tie him down, and at that age, it was enough to hold him. As the elephant grew, it was conditioned to believe it could not break away. The elephant believed the tiny rope could still hold him captive, so he never tried to break free. Sad to say, that is exactly how it is with many of us today, even when we are born again. That is why we need quickening, a fire in the belly that stirs that gifting within us so we can possess our possession.

Do you feel like there is more to life than you are currently experiencing? Do you feel like there is a divine purpose or calling for you to walk in? Do you feel that fire in your belly that something great needs to come out you? If you are experiencing any of these, then it is time for you to get clear on the will of God for your life. Remember, there is hope, and you can achieve all you think you can.

Getting Clear On The Will Of God For Your Life

But seek first the kingdom of God, and his righteousness, and all these things shall be added unto you. (Matthew 6:33 – KJV)

35

On the journey to possessing your possession, it is very important that you become clear what the will of God is for your life. Clarity gives you the opportunity to walk in the truth of who you really are and what it is you were created to do. You might ask: How do I discern the will of God for my life? What does getting clear on the will of God for my life look like? For me, it was spending time reading the Word of God, carving out prayer and journaling time, trusting the promptings of the Holy Spirit, examining my circumstances, and seeking Godly counsel.

Spending Time Reading The Word

One very important element on the road to possessing all that God has for you is to get into His Word. The Word of God gives us truth and is power-packed with the knowledge of the heart of God for us as believers. The Bible says, "For the word of God is living and powerful, and sharper than any two-edged sword, piercing even to the division of soul and spirit, and of joints and marrow, and is a discerner of the thoughts and intents of the heart." (Hebrews 4:12 - NKJV). The Bible shows us God's character and provides us God's revelation of Himself. It reveals to us God's holy, unchanging, faithful, gracious, and loving character so you can gain all the strategies required for you to navigate the complexities of life on the path to possessing your possession.

- The Word of God gives us **illumination** to bring light to the dark areas of our lives where we lack understanding. According to Psalm 119:130, "The unfolding of your words gives light; it imparts understanding to the simple." (ESV). The illumination through the Word can also be explored in Ephesians 1:18 where it mentioned, "having the eyes of your hearts enlightened, that you may know what is the hope to which he has called you, what are the riches of his glorious inheritance in the saints." (ESV).

- The Word of God gives us **instructions.** Psalm 32:8 says, "I will instruct you and teach you in the way you should go; I will counsel you with my eye upon you." (ESV). As you stay in the Word during the period of gaining clarity, the Word of God will give you instructions.

Carving Out Prayer And Journaling Time

Reading the Word is as important as praying back the Word of God. Prayer is so powerful that just the very act can shift the trajectory of one's life. The Bible says, according to Act 16:25-26, that at midnight "Paul and Silas prayed, and sang praises unto God: and the prisoners heard them. And suddenly there was a great earthquake, so that the foundations of the prison were shaken: and immediately all the doors were opened, and every one's bands were loosed." (KJV).

Prayer is so powerful that it can shake the foundations of an individual's life and lose the bands that have held you captive for years or decades. It is this shaking that is necessary to launch you in the path God has laid for you. My friend, it is critical that you know this: prayer links us to God, who is all-powerful, all-knowing and all-present. Prayer is not just wishful thinking. When we pray, we communicate directly with God, and our heart comes in alignment with the heart of God. This is what will bring manifestation and give you the ability to possess your possession.

When you pray, God instructs you on which path to take, whether it be in your personal lives, family, career or business. God is omnipotent; He can interrupt the natural laws of His creation to accomplish His will, if He chooses, so it is important you get to know His will for your life through prayer. If you are wondering what time of day is best for you to pray, the Bible gives us specific reference points when it comes to prayer.

Prayer Time

The Bible made special reference to three hours of prayer: the third, sixth and ninth hour of the day, or 9:00 A.M., 12 Noon, and 3:00 P.M. These were important prayer disciplines faithfully observed by the Old Testament saints, the New Testament Church, and by our Lord Jesus Christ. The hours of prayer were continually honored because they were divinely appointed. It is good to employ the system of praying without ceasing because the effectual fervent prayer of the righteous brings good results (see James 5:6). I would suggest that this strategy be employed for maximum success.

Jesus prayed early in the morning, according to Mark 1:35, "Very early in the morning, while it was still dark, Jesus got up, left the house and went off to a solitary place, where he prayed." (KJV). Paul and Silas prayed at midnight and angels of the Lord appeared. There was a mighty quake that shook the prison, and they were supernaturally released.

Daniel prayed three times per day. Daniel always prayed to God three times every day. Three times every day, he bowed down on his knees to pray and praise God. Even though Daniel heard about the new law, he still went to his house to pray. He went up to the upper room of his house and opened the windows that faced toward Jerusalem. Then Daniel bowed down on his knees and prayed just as he always had done (see Daniel 6:10).

Prayer is maintaining clear communication with God. Elijah knew this power through his battle with Jezebel's false prophets when he commanded fire to destroy them on Mount Carmel. He exercised the dominion and authority that was given to him by God, and through his commands, the rain came. This command is also given to us. When I was going through the process of defining my vision and discovering who I was called to be, I prayed early in the morning and waited to hear the instructions of the Holy Spirit. It was by praying and listening that I was

40

given secrets from the heart of God regarding His will for my life. I encourage you to pray and take your rightful place in the earth realm.

Examining Current Circumstances

As you pray and seek the Lord for clarity, you will notice that you are able to see things clearer in your life. You should now begin to look at your life and the things you have experienced over a lifespan of months or years. Your eyes will begin to open to things that are not in alignment with where the Lord is taking you and the ones that are. It is at this point that you will realize that the things that are not lined up with your purpose are a mere distraction.

God will never contradict Himself. He does not go back on His Word. God will never tell you to do something that is in violation of what His Word already says. Jeremiah 29:11 says, "For I know the plans I have for you," declares the Lord, "plans to prosper you and not to harm you, plans to give you hope and a future." (KJV).

As you analyze your life and current circumstances, take stock of your where you are. Look at the familiar mistakes you keep making year after year or season after season. Make a note of them so you can successfully avoid making the same error in your new season.

You will begin to see that even in your darkest of days, when you feel like giving up, there is a divine construction that is taking place by the One who has the master plan for your life.

Seek Godly Counsel/Advice

Proverbs 19:20 says, "Get all the advice and instruction you can, so you will be wise the rest of your life." (NLT). The wise man listens to godly advice, accepts instruction continually, and proactively seeks out wise counsel. According to Psalm 1:1, "Seek not counsel from the ungodly" (KJV) but seek Godly council from those seasoned saints who you know walk with the Lord.

There are so many platforms that are readily available to offer help in living your best life, etc. Social media is abuzz with them and, from the outside, the lives of these individuals seem so glamorous and one to be envied. But have you ever wondered why some of these same individuals commit suicide or are highlighted in the news for despicable acts? Have you ever wondered why there is no inner peace in the lives of these individuals, even with all the financial wealth they have accumulated? The Bible clearly illustrates that one of the obvious desires of God for His children is that we prosper and be in good health even as our souls prosper (see 3 John 1:2). One of the laws of good success and to be blessed is clearly outlined in Psalm 1:1-2 which says, "Blessed is the man that walketh not in the counsel of the ungodly nor stand in the way of sinners or sitteth in the seat of the scornful, but his delight is in the law of the Lord and in it doth he meditate day and night." (KJV). Additionally, Proverbs tells us, "Where there is no counsel the people fall, but in a multitude of counselors there is a safety." (Proverbs 11:14 – KJV). Without Godly counsel, you can easily get off course and make decisions that can prove to be detrimental to your destiny.

In leading the children of Israel to possess their possession, Joshua sought wise counsel from God which allowed him to defeat the giants in the land. However, in one instance, Joshua failed to consult God. The people in the land began to fear Israel because the Lord was helping them win all their battles. Because of this, the people in the town of

Gibeon knew the army was close and were afraid that Israel would attack them, so they played a trick and made themselves appear to have traveled a long way. They asked Joshua to make a treaty with them and promise to protect them. Joshua did not ask the Lord's advice but simply agreed to the treaty. When the Israelites later heard that the Gibeonites were neighbours, they knew they had been tricked. Even so, they knew they had to honour the treaty. When the enemies attacked Gibeon, Joshua took his army and protected Gibeon. The battle lasted a long time because the Lord caused the sun to stand still. Joshua did not consult God and was forced into a covenant with his enemies.

Not seeking wise counsel can lead you into ungodly covenants and even cause you to lose out on what was rightfully yours. The result of Joshua's hasty decision was that they could not fulfill God's command concerning all the inhabitants of the land. This is what happens when we fail to seek God's guidance. It results in us making bad decisions, just as Israel did. But rest assured, when we seek wise counsel, we can be thankful that God will guide us every step of the way, and we will be counted among the wise and not the fools who have rejected wise counsel and instructions.

Trust The Promptings Of The Holy Spirit

A key element on your journey is for you to trust the promptings of the Holy Spirit. It is important that you know for a fact that the Holy Spirit will speak to you and give you direction. He will teach and comfort you and bring to your remembrance those things He has set out for you. He will guide you into all truth about you. John 16:13 says, *"However, when the Spirit of truth comes, He will guide you into all truth. For He will not speak on His own, but He will speak what He hears, and He will declare to you what is to come." (NKJV).* The Holy Spirit is your connection to the heart and mind of God for your life. Therefore, when you trust His holy promptings, He will guide you on the path you should take.

You must first acknowledge that the Holy Spirit will speak to you and guide you as well as warn you about things to come. Secondly, it is important that you listen to the still, small voice and pay attention to the things you might inadvertently dismiss. Many times the blessings are planted in those things that are easily dismissed, so pay attention. Then set time to practice hearing how the Holy Spirit speaks to you. Following a spirit that is not of God is very detrimental to you reaching your final destination for your vision.

According to 1 John 4:1-3a, *"Beloved, do not believe every spirit, but test the spirits to see whether they are from God, for many false prophets have gone out into the world. By this you know the Spirit of God: every spirit that confesses that Jesus Christ has come in the flesh is from God, and every spirit that does not confess Jesus is not from God." (NIV).* Individuals are often led astray when they think they are following the Holy Spirit, but in actuality, they are simply following their own desires, some other person's desire for them, or a false spirit. If you find yourself boasting in your own abilities and not in the ability through Christ, know that you are being led astray.

When the Holy Spirit is speaking to you, it will be backed by the fruit of the Spirit. Anything that is contrary to this is a major red flag. According to Galatians 5:22-25, *"But the fruit of the Spirit is love, joy, peace, patience, kindness, goodness, faithfulness, gentleness, self-control; against such things there is no law. And those who belong to Christ Jesus have crucified the flesh with its passions and desires. If we live by the Spirit, let us also keep*

46

in step with the Spirit." (NIV). Stepping in the Spirit is where your steps are ordered by God. With this you can never fail or go offtrack. So, you may ask: How do I apply this in a practical way in my life? You may be speaking to the Holy Spirit about a major decision such as a marriage relationship, changing territories or even career as well as just your heart's desires. Please note that that conversation will always be centered around the fruit of the Spirit. God will show you how to have love, joy, peace, and all the other godly qualities in the specific area of your life that you are talking to Him about. God is not the author of confusion (see 1 Corinthians 14:33), so if you find that you are feeling confused, rushed, and off balance, you need to pay specific attention. There is abundance in God, so if you find yourself feeling like this is your last chance, and you must hastily make a decision that can potentially trap you or is detrimental to your destiny, stop! Always look for the peace of God in all you do.

You must pay attention and revisit so you are in joy, love, peace, self-control, and patience. In other words, whatever you sense the Holy Spirit speaking to you personally, you should be able to see those same truths, principles, and ideas in the Bible. In essence, when you carefully compare that which is

47

being presented to you or what you are hearing personally to what is already written in the Bible and the two match, you can be sure it is the Holy Spirit speaking to you.

There are examples in my life when the Holy Spirit spoke to me about certain directions to take and for me to understand what He was saying to me. The Lord started speaking to me audible when I was about fifteen years old. However, I was afraid at the time because I was naïve to the things of the Spirit. I could remember as a little girl going to Sunday school; I would hear the Holy Spirit telling me the scripture reading prior to me reaching church. I shared this with my mother a few times who laughed and thought it was funny. I would accurately know the scripture prior to reaching Church. Fast forward to my adult life, after rededicating my life to the Lord, I recognized that I would get a prompting to study a particular scripture during the week. When I arrived at church, the pastor would preach from the exact passage that I would be studying. This happened for many weeks consistently.

As youth director in the church, I was given the opportunity to preach the word on special occasions such as on a Youth Sunday. The Holy Spirit would

48

have it that when I needed encouragement in my spirit, someone would bring an exhortation with the exact message title I had researched, even though I didn't tell anyone about it. This happened for the entire time in ministry.

I remember one night after visiting church, I was at home alone because my children had gone on holiday and my house was very quiet. It was January 2017. I prayed to God the Wednesday night, and I told Him I needed to understand how He speaks to me. On the Saturday of that same week, I was washing the dishes when I heard a voice saying I should call Arlene— my friend from University whom I haven't spoken to in two years—and ask her how her husband was doing. I remember responding to the voice and saying, "I will call her and wish her a happy new year another time because I am hurrying to go pick up my children who are in the countryside with their grandparents." I heard the loud voice again, "Tracey, please call Arlene and ask her how her husband is doing." I remember answering yes to the voice, then I ran upstairs and picked up my phone. I dialed my friend's number; there was weeping and wailing on the line. I said, "May I please speak with Arlene?" Her daughter answered and said Arlene was crying right now because her husband just died. I started

49

crying too. I cried for Arlene and for how God showed up. This was a training ground for me on how to know when He is speaking to me.

During my time at University, the Holy Spirit would give me dreams and visions for subject areas to study prior to my exams. I would study, and if there was a particular area where I was struggling in, the Holy Spirit would give me a dream in the early morning for me to study.

With this experience, it was revealed to me that the Holy Spirit will train and teach you how to hear Him. In other words, whatever you sense the Holy Spirit speaking to you personally, you should be able to see them manifest through confirmation in the Bible as well. To gain an edge, you must dedicate the time for communion with Him. In addition, you will have a peace that surpasses human understanding, which will validate that in fact the Holy Spirit is speaking. Even in the midst of a storm in your life, you can have peace. Jesus Christ calmed the tempest and declared, "Peace be still!" The wind ceased, and there was a great calm. You have the power to declare peace over your situation, but it is important that you are being led by the Holy Spirit.

PHASE 2:

WRITE THE VISION

Then the LORD answered me and said: "Write the vision and make it plain on tablets, that he may run who reads it." (Habakkuk 2:2 – KJV)

By now, you would have had your "aha" moment where you know there is something more for you to do; you feel destiny calling and purpose is bubbling within you. You have set yourself to get clear by spending time praying and seeking Godly counsel, as well as developing your relationship to hear the voice of the Holy Spirit, who is your ultimate Guide. It is now time for you to engage in a very spiritual act. This is the act of writing the vision. The Bible, in Habakkuk 2:2, makes it clear that we must *"write the vision and make it plain"* that those who are involved would get in the mode of taking action for it to come to pass. So, what is the definition of vision: *A vision is a desired long-term outcome that should be clearly articulated that those who are involved (your inner circle) will understand the meaning and purpose and be engaged in its implementation. It can be considered your final destination or the end state of where you want to go.* A written vision will provoke accountability from yourself and those key people such as family and very close friends. We see in the Bible where the Lord instructed Moses, "Write this

52

down on a scroll as a permanent reminder." (Exodus 7:14 - NKJV). He also encouraged Jeremiah to write all the words that was spoken to him of the Lord in a book (see Jeremiah 30:1). The Bible, in Psalm 105:5, articulates that we should "remember" the wonders God has done. Psalm 103:2 tells us to bless the Lord and "forget not" all his benefits. So, we see that if the Lord is instructing us to write, it is because it helps us to remember those important elements of our journey.

We are humans and we do forget, and for this reason, we should be writing important things such as our visions that we do not forget. In addition, writing things down will serve as a reference as it gives us something for us to work with the Holy Spirit. Many times, the Holy Spirit will send me back to my journal for me to find things that He spoke to me years ago that I have forgotten.

In designing your vision, it requires consultation from God and communicating with/translation to your family and close associates. God should be the director of your vision. It is therefore necessary that in your time of gaining clarity on the strategy of how to possess your possession, that you write those key things that the Holy Spirit is instructing you to do. It

53

is very unfortunate that many individuals are still operating without a written vision. They expect to see manifestation; however, there is no written vision guiding them. It can also be frustrating when you have a fire in your belly for greatness but are unaware of the steps to implementation. It is therefore necessary for you to have a written vision that is backed by God. There are several components of your vision that you need to be mindful of:

- Your vision is sent from God.
- Your vision should be clear—it has clarity/is plain and easy to understand.
- Your vision should be visible to you and those close to you.
- Your vision is for a set time.
- Your vision must be articulated.
- Your vision must be protected.
- Your vision must be planned for.
- Your vision should be met with expectation, prepared for manifestation.
- Your vision should be prioritized and prayed over.
- Your vision is your guiding light in times of difficulty.

On your path to possessing your possession, execution of your vision requires that you have goals. Goals are smaller bite-size pieces of activities that will incrementally add to you achieving your overarching vision. George T. Doran introduced the SMART goal concept back in 1981 to help individuals improve the chances of succeeding in accomplishing a broader outcome. In this case it is our vision. I have found that the SMART principle has helped me tremendously in going after my personal vision. The principle means that the goals you set should meet the criteria of being S.M.A.R.T:

- Specific
- Measurable
- Attainable
- Relevant
- Time bound

I remembered in 2017 when I set myself to seek the Lord for direction in my life. It was a time of solitude where I would read the Word and spend time to hear the Spirit of God speak to me. The Holy Spirit told me to write all that He has placed on my heart. At the time I was actively journaling, and as I wrote, I would get divine revelation. I wanted to build my house at the time, and I didn't see how I would be able to finance such an endeavor as a single parent. The Lord said to me that I should write what I wanted the house to be like and He would bring it to pass. I also got pictures similar to the desires that God had placed in my heart and placed them all around my bedroom where I would be able to see them day and night. As I looked at those pictures everyday, my focus expanded, and I started seeing opportunities that would eventually lead me in the path of individuals that would favor me in building my house. I prayed over those photos and declared that my house was built. In my mind's eye, I would see myself cooking, cleaning, and gardening in my new home. I literally felt the real presence of being in my home every day and every night, and God sent me supernatural help. That project took off so fast; all I could do was offer a prayer of thanksgiving. By 2018, my house was built, and I was able to move into my own home that once seemed impossible.

The principles I applied were in line with the SMART principles, but I also had my vision board visible where I would daily pray over and declare it was coming to pass. I have also used this method for many other things in my life, such as moving to Canada. I saw myself in the cities, riding on the train, going on excursions; as I saw those things in my mind's eye, I also felt it, and they have all come to pass. I encourage you to have your vision clearly written and visible where you can see it, pray over it, and declare, "It is done." Never share your vision with envious individuals; these are the people who can actually kill your vision. You must protect it! Make your vision a priority and prepare for the manifestation of your vision.

Put Order To Your Finances

For which of you, intending to build a tower, does not sit down first and count the cost, whether he has enough to finish it. (Luke 14:28 – KJV)

At this point, you should have a clearer perspective of where you intend to journey to possess your vision. We know that without a vision we will end up anywhere, and we should eliminate that at all costs. Another important element to consider is that of your financial standing. It is now time to set your financial house in order. In one of His parables, Jesus asked the question in Luke 14:28, *"For which of you intending to build a tower, does not sit down first and count the cost, whether he has enough to finish it." (KJV)*. I strongly believe this is also true for you as you embark on your path to possession. It is

57

important that you do the costing for your journey, and even though you might not have the money at the outset, there are things you need to put in place in order to mitigate any blockages that may delay your progress.

Financial management is very important on your path to success. It is the responsible thing to do in the sight of God. The Bible, in Proverbs 21:5, tells us that the plans of the diligent lead to profit as surely as haste leads to poverty. 1 Timothy 5:8 says, "But if anyone does not provide for his relatives, and especially for members of his household, he has denied the faith and is worse than an unbeliever." (NIV). We see in Proverbs 13:22 that "good people leave an inheritance to their grandchildren, but the sinner's wealth passes to the godly." (NIV).

So, when we talk about managing your finances, what do we really mean? What does it look like?

1. **Seek Wise Financial Counsel** – You can get information from your Financial Advisor at your local bank. You can seek online courses to help you in the area of financial literacy. And, very importantly, read the Bible. It is

packed with financial wisdom that can guide you.

2. **Work on your credit** and eliminate any high interest loans or debt that you have accumulated.

3. **Do a budget and stick to it** - A budget is a financial plan for a defined period, often one year. It may also include planned sales volumes and revenues, resource quantities, costs and expenses, assets, liabilities, and cash flows. Have a simple budget to guide your spending.

4. **Save 1/10 of your earnings** - Saving is setting aside money you don't spend now for emergencies or for future purchases. Put some money aside to help with the plans to achieve your vision.

5. **Save for emergencies** – Plan ahead of unforeseen events, such as accidents, car troubles, sickness, etc. Think about how much should be in your emergency fund. Most financial institutions encourage that you should have between three to six months of

your household income on hand at all times to deal with unforeseen emergencies.

6. **Give (tithing)** – Giving is a spiritual law, and when you give, rest assured that it will be given back to you. The Bible encourages you to give and it shall be given to you in good measure, pressed down, shaken together and running over will men pure into your bosom (see Luke 6:38).

7. **Seek out multiple sources of income. Analyze your abilities.** Ecclesiastes 11:1-2 says, "Cast your bread upon the waters, for after many days you will find it again. Divide your portion among seven, or even eight, for you do not know what disaster may befall the land." (BSB). Analyze your abilities, look at what else you can do. Can you write? Can you style hair? Do you have a skill that you can strengthen? These are areas you can strengthen in order to build your finances.

8. **Be content** – When you are content with your life, it will eliminate a mindset of want, and you will focus on what you need instead. You

will be less likely to become indebted by keeping up with the Jones.

9. **Be a good steward** - While you embark on organizing your finances, you must recognize that you are the manager of what God has given to you and not the owner. When you manage what has been given to you, then more will be given to you.

Growing Yourself Out Of Debt

On the path to possess your promises, if you find yourself in a situation where you are indebted, do not give up. There is hope for you even if you are deep in debt. The Bible gives us an assurance in Deuteronomy 28:1-2, which says, "Now it shall come to pass, if you diligently obey the voice of the LORD your God, to observe carefully all His commandments which I command you today, that the LORD your God will set you high above all nations of the earth. And all these blessings shall come upon you and overtake you, because you obey the voice of the LORD your God." (KJV). You can get out of debt if you listen and follow the instructions of the Lord pertaining to your finances.

1. Commit your finances to the Lord and He will bring all you need to pass. The Bible says, according to Proverbs 16:3, "Commit to the LORD whatever you do, and he will establish your plans." (NIV). This is also the case with your finances.

2. Do self-assessment. Know and understand why you are in debt in the first place. Heal your emotional relationship with your finances and agree to live by God's principles. Seek to know what God has to say to you in your situation. Be absolutely honest about your faults and mistakes to prevent similar future scenarios. Obey the spiritual law "Give, and it will be given to you: good measure, pressed down, shaken together, and running over will be put into your bosom. For with the same measure that you use, it will be measured back to you." (Luke 6:38 – KJV).

3. Set a realistic budget and stick to it. Spending more than you have is a sure way to go into poverty—you should seek your financial advisor or get a simple template online. It means you will have to cut out unnecessary

spending for a while, for example, eating out or buying excess clothing.

4. Debt consolidation - Seek help from your Financial Advisor. You can use this for high interest payment such as credit cards. First, look at the individual interest rates you are currently being charged on your high-interest, unsecured debts. You want to make sure the debt consolidation loan has a lower interest rate than the average interest rate you are currently paying on your debts.

5. Pay off credit card on time. If you have a credit card, pay off the credit within thirty days of using it. This can be like a 0% loan if you can manage it properly. Otherwise, it can be like a death trap. Be very wise.

6. Snowball effects—the debt snowball method by David Ramsey is a debt-reduction strategy where you pay off debts in order of smallest to largest, gaining momentum as you knock out each remaining balance. When the smallest debt is paid in full, you roll the minimum payment you were making on that debt into the next, smallest debt payment.

7. Give yourself a timeline and work within your plan and be content with it.

8. Save—even in growing yourself out of debt. It is important to set aside some money to build your saving portfolio.

9. Maintain laser-focus, discipline, and pray always.

Coming Into Agreement With God's Desire

Another important key that is required to possess your possessions is the covenant with God's desire. A covenant is defined as a formal, solemn, and binding agreement between two or more parties. It is critical to know that from the beginning of time God has been in the covenant-making business. Genesis 1:26 says: *"And God said; Let us make man in our image, after our likeness: and let them have dominion over the fish of the sea, and over the fowl of the air, and over the cattle, and over all the earth, and over every creeping thing that creepeth upon the earth." (KJV).*

It is God's will for man to have dominion. There is power when you come into agreement/alignment with your vision and the desire God has placed in your heart. Agreement is vital for manifestation. The question was asked in Amos 3:3, "Can two walk together, except they be agreed?" (KJV). When you agree to pursue your vision, you are making a commitment in the spirit that will propel you into manifestation. Agreement requires that you must shift your mindset to align with that which you seek.

Coming into agreement means you are fully sold out to your vision, and you desire the desire God has placed in your heart. Agreement means you are committing time, energy, and resources to bring your vision to pass. It also means you are being intentional, and you can assess, based on the activities you are doing, if you are in alignment or if you are straying. At this point, every decision you make should be propelling you one step closer to your vision. Agreement is you working with an end state in mind, and that end state is your broader vision. Without an end state in mind, you will likely give up in challenging times. A solid vision that is agreed to can be your guiding light in difficulty. Proverbs 29:18 states, "Without a vision the people perish; but he that keepeth the law, happy is he." (KJV).

Ask God to grant you the desires of your heart. In Matthew 7:7-8, it is highlighted that we should "**Ask, and it shall be given you; seek, and ye shall find**; knock, and it shall be opened unto you: For every one that asketh receiveth; and he that seeketh findeth; and to him that knocketh it shall be opened." (KJV – emphasis mine). Extend your faith and ask God for big things. Step out in faith. According to your faith, be it onto you, for whatever you allow on earth is allowed in heaven; therefore, get out of agreement with things that do not suit you and align with your purpose.

Eliminate Plan B

You might be wondering what eliminating plan B has to do with your journey to possess your possession. Let me tell you this: Plan B can be defined as a person, place, thing or opportunity that you go to should plan A fail. It is your fallback plan, your safe place, your comfort zone. It signals that there is a need for safety for something to run back to. It sends the message that there might be a possibility of plan A failing. In 1 Kings 19, we see Elijah falling into depression and brokenness after his battle with the Baal prophets. God reassures him by sending His angels to speak hope that he was not alone. The angels provided refreshments and gave him instructions on several things to do. One of those tasks was to anoint his successor, Elisha.

Elijah found Elisha as a farmer, plowing in a field. Elijah threw his mantle upon Elisha, beckoning the call to a new way of life. At first, when Elijah tapped Elisha, Elisha expressed interest, but he asked permission to say "Goodbye" first. In the moment of saying goodbye, he threw himself a celebration party. He killed his twelve oxen. Then he broke up their yoke and his plowing equipment to build a fire. He roasted the meat and fed the people. Once everyone had eaten, Elisha left and followed Elijah. This act is worth noting on your journey to possess your possession. Elisha "burnt his bridges" with farming, which was his original profession. For him, there was no turning back, no plan B, no fallback plan. He burnt his farming equipment and all his oxen. How profound!

When Jesus called Peter, Andrew, James, and John, they left their boats and followed Him. But they didn't destroy their boats. In fact, they still used their boats after becoming Jesus' disciples. After Jesus died, some went back to the livelihood of fishing. Since their boats were still available, they had a backup plan. Elisha did not have a fallback option. When he decided to follow Elijah, he killed his oxen and destroyed his equipment. He burnt his bridges— he eliminated plan B. He had no work to return to if things didn't work out with Elijah and the call to become a prophet. He had no opportunity to go back. He was committed—he was all in.

God wants us to be committed to Him, to go all in, and with no option to return to what we left behind. He wants us to do His will and to follow that call He has placed on us. He wants us to walk in agreement with His will for our lives. With Jesus, there should be no turning back.

Plan B is the signal that there is little faith, belief or conviction that you are capable of achieving that great vision. With this mindset, you have set off in the realm of the spirit that you are not fully committed to your vision. Eliminating plan B is critical for you to achieve plan A. Thought becomes things, and whatever you focus on, you get more of; therefore, on your journey to destiny, if you are constantly focusing on your fallback plan, it will take away from the energy you should be putting into your main plan. Plan B can set you up to be double-minded. In essence, your focus on your fallback plan

B is confirming your lack of faith and also your fears as it relates to making the big, bold action step of faith.

It can be proven that people perform better when there is no safety net. The absence of a safety net means you have no choice but to commit to ensuring that your purpose plan A is fulfilled. The Bible says that faith is the substance of things hoped for, the evidence of things not seen (see Hebrew 11:1).

Another case in point is with Father Abraham. Abraham, the father of many nations, did not stagger in his faith. When the Lord told him to leave the land of his birth, Ur of the Chaldeans, and go to the promised land that was prepared for him, I am sure he must have wondered about leaving such a lucrative place. His hometown was one of the greatest cities in the ancient world. Ur was the capital of the ancient Chaldean Empire in ancient Mesopotamia. Nevertheless, Abraham had unwavering faith and went with his family and took the journey that would take him through seventeen stops and finally ended in the land of Canaan.

If we want to manifest, we must believe it is already done. We must put away unbelief. We must be fully persuaded, trusting in the Lord with all our hearts and lean not to our own understanding, but in all our ways, acknowledge Him, and he will direct our path in following plan A.

Manifestation takes faith, hope, and belief. If you have faith as small as a mustard seed, nothing is impossible (see Matthew 17:20). According to Hebrews 11:11, *"Through faith, Sara herself also received strength to conceive seed; and was delivered of child when she was past age; because she judged him faithful who had promised." (KJV).* Hope is linked to manifestations, and without hope, there is no faith. Hope is your expectation. If you pray and believe, you will receive. It is important that you are operating in the realm of faith, hope, and belief in order to receive.

Limiting Belief Blocks Manifestation

When Paul wrote that we should be transformed by the renewing of our minds (see Romans 12:2), he knew quite well the link to manifestation. If we have limiting belief, it is impossible for us to receive what God has already given to us. What you see is what you get. If you have belief that is not aligned with what the Word of God says about your life, then you will not receive it.

At the age of thirty-eight, the Holy Spirit prompted me to retire from my Senior Director position at the Government of Jamaica. He told me to resign from my role. He told me that for this new phase of my life, I needed to extend a greater faith. My wonderful dream job in Government, working with the United Nations, and the freedom to travel was now plan B. It was my comfort zone that if I had stayed there, I could retire well with no stress. When I resigned, I had no option but to go after what God had called me to be. I had nothing to look back to, just as Elisha. Being a single mother with three young children, it did not seem like the responsible thing to leave my job. Nothing in the natural was making sense. If I had held on to my comfort zone, it meant I would not leave, and I would have forfeited this new thing the Lord was calling me into.

Letting go of plan B means you now have to put all your efforts into achieving plan A. I moved to Canada, and God provided me with signs and wonders. He has taken care of us and provided in tremendous ways. Many opportunities came to me that could have only been by His design. When I moved to Alberta, Canada, I did not know what my future would be like. Literally, I had no support system when I decided to move into the unknown, but with God in the vessel, rest assured, you can smile at the storm. God provided a new family for me and new faith-believing friends who supported my journey. I had no idea there were people already being provided for me, but there were. When you step out in faith, God is sure to honor your move. Rest assured, you will not be put to shame.

So, now I asked the question, Do you want to see a change? If you do, then take that jump and watch God catch you. Take that bold leap of faith, that big action step of faith, so God can change the world through you. Remember that what God has in store for you is greater than you can ever imagine. God will do exceedingly abundantly than we can ever ask, think or imagine (see Ephesian 3:20). Trust God completely; you do not have a choice.

God will sometimes make that thing we idolize disappear from us. It could be a job, marriage, house, car, and other relationships. He will take it away from us so we can completely trust Him. Do not be like the one who trusts in chariots and horses. Trust in the name of God.

72

The real reason some people go for plan B is because of the thought of worry. Worry can overtake the mind when there is a focus on us failing. The mind feels safe and will fall back to its comfort zone. This place of plan B can be very dangerous to destiny. It means that the faith is weak and needs to be strengthened.

Faith is knowing without a shadow of a doubt that this vision, desire, and goal will manifest if you put in the work and let the sovereign Lord take charge. Remember on your journey that the greater the action step of faith, the greater you will see the manifestation of the will of God's glory in your life. Do not be afraid of failing at your 1st, 2nd, 3rd, or even 100th attempt for the thing which you are seeking to achieve. Thomas Edison made 10,000 unsuccessful attempts before winning in getting the light bulb. Being stuck on plan B is idealizing and idolizing failure. Whatever you focus on expands; therefore, you are attracting more of "I am afraid to go wholeheartedly to plan A." In the realm of the spirit, it is signaling a lack of faith that is required to propel you into destiny. Once the decision is made, it is important that you take the action steps towards realizing your vision.

Strategies To Strengthen Your Faith For Manifestation of Plan A

- Know and remind yourself that you are saved by hope.

- Know that the Spirit also helpeth our infirmities, for when we know not what to pray for as we ought, the Spirit itself maketh intercessions for us with groaning which cannot be uttered. (see Romans 8:26).

- He that searcheth the hearts knoweth what is in the mind of the Spirit, because He maketh intercession for us in groaning which cannot be uttered according to the will of God. (see Romans 8:27).

- We know that all things work together for good to them that love God, to them who are the called according to His purpose. (see Romans 8:28).

- Know that if God is for you, nothing can be against you.

- Now step out in faith.

Tap Into The Power Of Belief

For verily I say unto you, that whosoever shall say unto this mountain, Be thou removed, and be thou cast into the sea; and shall not doubt in his heart, but shall believe that those things which he saith shall come to pass; he shall have whatsoever he saith. (Mark 11:23 - KJV)

As you trod, possess, occupy, and dominate, it is important that you fully understand the power there is in belief. According to the dictionary definition, belief is something that is accepted as true. In Hebrew, the meaning of belief (bə'lēf) is trust, faith, or confidence in someone or something. The Bible gives us many instances where Jesus spoke to His disciples about belief. In Mark 11, we see where Jesus cursed the fig tree for not bearing fruit, and as His disciples remembered that action from the day before, Jesus reiterated to them that they should "Have faith in God." Mark 11:23 says, *"Truly I tell you that if anyone says to this mountain, 'Be lifted up and thrown into the sea,' and has no doubt in his heart but believes that it will happen, it will be done for him. Therefore I tell you, whatever you ask for in prayer, believe that you have received it, and it will be yours." (KJV).*

The Lord Jesus says once you believe when you pray and doubt not, you will receive the answer. On your journey, I want to encourage you that it is vital that you believe in your vision and that it is God's will for you to possess the promise. You have prayed, and you have received the confirmation in so many ways. It is now time for you to believe and take the step of faith.

When Jesus spoke to His disciples about the mountain, it was symbolic of the issues and struggles of life that come to make us doubt. It is synonymous with the problems we face. Now, if we walk in the power of belief, we can speak to those mountains, issues, and problems. Our words are so powerful that once we say it and doubt not, the problems must flee from us. It is important that when you encounter these challenges, that you have a strong belief that you are overcoming them day by day. These could be mountains in the form of relationships, health, finances, career, etc. Whatever you are believing God for, believe it is already done unto you. If you are experiencing challenges, speak to it and believe what God says. Examples of affirmations that I believe:

- I shall possess my possession.

76

- No weapon that is formed against me shall prosper.
- Sickness and diseases are far from me.
- If God be for me, no one can be against me.

Now get some biblical affirmations pertaining to your issues and speak them over your life; believe and you will see the manifestation.

**Allow someone with strong faith
to believe for you so you can see the
manifestation of your vision.**

If you are experiencing doubt, you can ask someone to believe for you. Did you know that the faith of a family member, friend, or spiritual leader can help you manifest your vision? Yes, they can believe for you. This principle was active in Matthew 8 when the centurion approached Jesus for a miracle for one of his servants. It was the faith of the Centurion that brought healing to his servant. Being a man of authority, he understood that Jesus had the power to command any sickness to leave. With this knowledge, the Centurion went to Jesus believing for a miracle for his servant. As soon as Christ heard of the servant's serious condition and detected the centurion's humility and faith, Jesus said, "Go your

77

way; and as you have believed, so let it be done for you." (Matthew 8:13 - KJV). The healing occurred immediately. It did not take months or weeks or days; he was healed that same hour. This miracle shows that someone can have faith for you that will allow for the healing, breakthrough, and manifestation of your vision.

In the book of Matthew 18:19, Jesus Christ says if two or more people agree on anything that they ask, it will be done for them by His Father in heaven.

"Again I say unto you, That if two of you shall agree on earth as touching any thing that they shall ask, it shall be done for them of my Father which is in heaven." (Matthew 18:19 - KJV).

It is important that you have prayer support. I have a group of twelve that I pray with on a regular basis. Whenever I have a specific issue that I might be struggling with as it relates to my belief, I engage in prayer with my partners, and the person who is strong in that area takes the lead. For example, I have manifested many scholarships in my lifetime in the form of my 1st and 2nd degree, plus numerous certifications because I exercised my faith in this area. It is very easy for me to believe for someone who is expecting manifestation in this area of higher education and scholarships. Someone else who has a very good relationship can believe for you to manifest the same thing in prayer. In essence, you can have someone who has great faith in a particular area pray and believe for you. This is a sure way to manifest your dreams, visions, and desires.

As you continue on the journey, remember that it will be onto you according to your belief. I encourage you to eliminate self-doubt and not waiver as you step out in faith to see the manifestation of the vision God has carved out for you.

Maintain Laser Focus: Eliminate Procrastination and Distractions

Now you have decided to stick to the vision, and you are fully committed to the path. You have been through the defining process and have come into full agreement/alignment of where you are going on this journey to possess your possession. You must now maintain laser focus in order to eliminate procrastination and those things that will delay your manifestation. Focus means you are looking ahead. The vision is already set, and this new vision should now be your point of focus. Refrain from looking back on the many failures you had in the past. Only use your failures as a launching pad to push you to your potential. Remember, you are now a new creation. Old thoughts are passed away. This vision was developed with you and God. The Holy Spirit has downloaded everything that is possible for you to obtain. This is not about following the tribe; this is a spirit-led mission. It now requires you to focus on that vision or goal that is in line with the purpose God has created for you from before the foundation of the world.

It is important to note that the human brain is amazingly complex and powerful. It is commonly believed that humans, on average, use only a small percentage of their brain's capacity. However, when we mobilize our power of thought towards a single issue for a prolonged time, we can achieve spectacular results. So it is when we focus on achieving the tasks that are in line with us achieving our God-given vision.

Maintaining focus gives power to the expansion of new ideas that will flow from the realm of creativity. Unfortunately, some people's thinking is often scattered, flitting from one thought to the next without ever settling on one topic long enough. This

80

flitting will take away the energy that could otherwise be used to build momentum essential for manifestation. Staying focused on the most important topic at hand until it is resolved takes willpower and, if not managed correctly, can delay us on the path to destiny.

Pick a priority action item from your implementation plan and work on it until it is completed. It is far better to have two finished tasks than seven incomplete. Set your time to work through the task and eliminate all distractions, and you will see yourself moving closer to the manifestation of your vision.

PHASE 3:

THE TROD – THE STRATEGY

Every Place that the sole of your foot shall tread upon, that have I give unto you as I said unto Moses. (Joshua 1:3 – KJV)

The real walk has begun. Where are you going? What are you doing? Remember, your vision is your guidepost, but you need a strategy that will guide its implementation. Every action step that you have taken, you will manifest. Are you going back to school, getting that certificate, opening that business, or writing that book? As stated in Joshua 1:3, every place that you have set out to dominate by the will of God you will possess.

In this chapter, I will look at the blueprint for possessing your possession using time-tested biblical principles that have also helped me in walking in the promises God has for me. A strategy can be defined as a plan of action or policy designed to achieve a major or overall aim. Words and phrases synonymous with strategy are *master plan, grand design, game plan, plan of action, plan, policy, proposed action, scheme, blueprint, program, procedure, approach, schedule, tactics, set of tactics, and process.* Everything from this point onwards will align with the vision or greater purpose.

Take Action, Get Up And Go!

So, you have done your research, and you have analyzed the place where you want to go. You have agreed to God's directing you; you have spent time getting clear with the help of the Holy Spirit, you have watched all the videos, took all the training and read all the books. So now what? Now that you have gathered all the knowledge required, it is time you get up and go. Getting up and going is synonymous with making a decision and taking action. There is something special about being ready to take action. According to world-renowned artist, Pablo Picasso, "Action *is the fundamental key to all success."* You will not be able to walk into your promises if you are not ready to take action.

Taking action is the most important step towards achieving your vision. The simple truth is that dreams, visions, and goals are achieved and accomplished only through action. Being ready means you are prepared mentally and physically to take on an experience or an action. The Lord spoke to Joshua and said, "Get ready, Joshua, *arise and go!"*

Moses my servant is dead. Now then, you and all these people, get ready to cross the Jordan River into

85

the land I am about to give to them—to the Israelites.
(Joshua 1:2 – NIV).

The experience in this scenario was in light of possessing the promised land that was given to the children of Israel. For you to be ready, it also signals that you are in agreement.

"After the death of the Lord's servant Moses, the Lord said to Moses' helper, Joshua the son of Nun, 'My servant Moses is dead. So you and all these people get up and cross the Jordan River to the land I am giving to the people of Israel. I have given you every place where the bottom of your foot steps, as I promised Moses. Your land will be from the desert and from Lebanon as far as the big Euphrates River. It will be all the land of the Hittites to the Great Sea on the west. No man will be able to stand against you all the days of your life. I will be with you just as I have been with Moses. I will be faithful to you and will not leave you alone. Be strong and have strength of heart. For you will bring the people in to take this land which I promised to their fathers to give them. Only be strong and have much strength of heart. Be careful to obey all the Law which My servant Moses told you. Do not turn from it to the right or to the left. Then all will go well with

86

you everywhere you go. This book of the Law must not leave your mouth. Think about it day and night, so you may be careful to do all that is written in it. Then all will go well with you. You will receive many good things. Have I not told you? Be strong and have strength of heart! Do not be afraid or lose faith. For the Lord your God is with you anywhere you go.'" (Joshua 1:1- 9 – NLV).

Joshua was encouraged to take possession of the land that was given to the children of Israel. What if he had decided not to go? He would not have seen success. So it is with us today, no matter the knowledge and the endorsement we have regarding our potential or the next step in our lives, if we do not take the actions necessary, we will not see the manifestation.

There Is Power In Starting

In taking action, it is important for us to examine the following: Examine what is needed to take action. What are the resources we need to take this action step? Is it going back to school? What are the credits that I need? How much money will it take? How much of the resources do I have, and how much do I still need? Luke 14:28 says, *"For which of you, desiring to build a tower, does not first sit down and count the cost, whether he has enough to complete it?" (ESV).*

Clearly outline the key steps of action. Make a plan, and determine when you will move to execute the plan.

Prepare yourself for the journey. Prepare mentally and physically for the journey. Preparation is also one of the key elements required to be successful.

Action also allows you to build your faith Muscle. When you jump off into the deep, heaven conspires to assist you. Also, one action step of faith will propel you to an even larger action step of faith, and this is where you will see the manifestation of God's operation in your life.

Spy Out The Land: Analysis, The Plan, What You Need, Your Resources, The People

On your path to possessing your possession, one of the key steps is that of doing an analysis or research of where you desire to go. This is what businesses or organizations refer to as strategic analysis where they use various approaches such as PESTEL Model (political, economical, socio-cultural, technological, environmental, and legal scenario) or a SWOT analysis, examining strengths, weakness, opportunities, and threats of the environment. We see from the Bible that Moses was way ahead of his time. In Numbers 13, Moses sent men to spy out the land of Canaan which was given to his people by the Lord.

Moses sent them to spy out the land of Canaan. He said to them, "Go up there into the Negev. Then go up into the hill country. See what the land is like. See if the people who live in it are strong or weak, and if they are few or many. Find out if the land they live in is good or bad. See if the cities they live in are open or if they have walls. Find out if the land is rich or poor, and if there are trees in it or not. Then try to get some of the fruit of the land." Now this was the gathering time of the first grown grapes. (Numbers 13:17–20 – NLV).

From this scripture we can clearly see all the elements of the PESTEL analysis at play. Moses wanted to know what the environment, economy, and socio-culture were like. He wanted to know about the people. *Is the land fruitful?*

We can see where the SWOT analysis is similar to Moses' analysis. He wanted to know the strengths and weaknesses of the people. He wanted to know about the cities, if they had walls or were open. A closed city would be able to mitigate a threat more easily than an open city. This would let him know how to launch his attack. It can be interpreted from this strategy that an environmental scan or spying is vital prior to entering the promised land. Moses instructed his men to do an analysis and report back the findings. This analysis or research will prepare you for success. If you are to dominate, you must be very familiar with your environment.

Now I want you to set aside some time and think about your vision. Write out the things that will be required for you on your journey. For those of you who have been called to go into new territories, get all the information about the place where you want to live and be specific. List your area of strength and see how best to align those to where you want to go. This will enable you to have an understanding of what you need to strengthen in order to succeed.

Moses wanted evidence; he told them to pick the fruits of the trees. This lets him know that the land the people are entering is a fruitful land. He wanted to know if it was a place where the people could thrive. So will it be with us. We need the evidence, and that is why it is important for us to do our analysis. Your analysis will equip you with information on how to navigate. It will allow you to put the necessary plans in place and forms an integral part of your preparation.

The Power Of Being Prayerful: Having Faith

Romans 10:17 - "So faith comes from hearing, and hearing through the word of Christ." (ESV).

"Faith comes by hearing and hearing the word of God." (KJV). Developing faith is critical on the path to possessing your possession. After you have done your analysis and taken action to get up and pursue that dream, goal, or desire, it is vitally important for you to cultivate faith that will enable you to be sustained. You will have challenges on the path to your possession; there will be giants in the land; you will have walls that are in front of you, but the key in overcoming these blockages is the faith that you possess.

The Lord commanded Joshua that the book of the law should not leave out of his mouth. He told him to

91

have strength in his heart. You must understand that once it is spoken out of the mouth, it will also be heard. So it is when you mediate and read the Word of God. You will hear it, and it will strengthen your faith. Once you are convinced that you are walking in the will of God for your life, you must remember the Word of the Lord. He said he will never leave or forsake you (see Hebrews 13:5); He said He will keep you in perfect peace if your mind is stayed on Him (see Isaiah 26:3). Remember that the Lord has given the promises, and no matter how it might seem, you need to hold on to that word. Know also that fear is the opposite of faith. When the enemy or circumstances present itself to cause fear on you, it is vital that you use the weapon of faith to keep your place. You will also build your faith by taking action. When you have stepped out in faith, that first step of faith will help you move on to the next, and so on. By the time you realize it, it will be like a compounded effect.

So How Do You Practice Faith?

- Study the Word of God. The Lord commanded Joshua, "This book of the law should not depart from your mouth."

- Set positive affirmations, meditate on the word, and repeat it back yourself until it is embedded in your subconscious mind.

- Build your faith muscle by stepping out and taking action.

- Put into practice what you have read.

- Being prayerful always.

The Power Of Being With The Right People: The Master Mind

Another important element on the road to possessing your possession is having the right people in your corner. Exposure to the right people will allow you to see from a different perspective. Hang around the people who represent the possibility of where you are going.

The Bible highlights in Proverbs 11:14, *Where there is no guidance, a people falls, but in an abundance of counselors there is safety (ESV)*. Napoleon Hill clearly articulates this in his principle of a mastermind: *"two or more minds working actively together in perfect harmony toward a common definite object."* World-renowned Auto Innovator, Henry Ford, applied this principle by surrounding himself with advisors who were knowledgeable in key critical areas for his business development: "Through his association with Edison, Burbank, Burroughs, and Firestone, Mr. Ford added to his own brain power the sum and substance of the intelligence, experience, knowledge, and spiritual forces of these four men." **(Napoleon Hill, Think and Grow Rich).**

So, it is with your walk on your path to the promise. The Bible says in Proverbs 13:20 - *"Whoever walks with the wise becomes wise, but the companion of fools will suffer harm." (ESV). Ecclesiastes 4:9-12 also says, "Two are better than one, because they have a good reward for their toil. For if they fall, one will lift up his fellow. But woe to him who is alone when he falls and has not another to lift him up! Again, if two lie together, they keep warm, but how can one keep warm alone? And though a man might prevail against one who is alone, two will withstand him—a threefold cord is not quickly broken." (ESV).* This reiterates your need for alliances or network.

In Joshua 2, we see the power of alliance with the spies and Rahab.

94

Joshua 2:3-6 states: "So the king of Jericho sent this message to Rahab: "Bring out the men who came to you and entered your house, because they have come to spy out the whole land. But the woman had taken the two men and hidden them. She said, "Yes, the men came to me, but I did not know where they had come from. At dusk, when it was time to close the city gate, they left. I don't know which way they went. Go after them quickly. You may catch up with them." But she had taken them up to the roof and hidden them under the stalks of flax she had laid out on the roof." (KJV).

We see the implication of an alliance with Rahab, the harlot. On your journey to possessing your possession, be discerning of people. Surround yourself with the right people. Be mindful of who you allow to occupy your time. Ask God to bring the right people to you and open your eyes to see the things He is calling you into. Also, remember, sometimes your destiny helpers are not packaged as you would expect. Do not reject your helpers because of their packaging (i.e., attire, profession, or status in life). Be discerning!

Be Aware Of The Gibeonite Spirit

We have seen the power of being with the right people, but we also need to be cognizant of the fact that being with the wrong people can be equally destructive. The Bible illustrates in the book of Joshua 9: *"Now when all the kings west of the Jordan heard about these things—the kings in the hill country, in the western foothills, and along the entire coast of the Mediterranean Sea as far as Lebanon (the kings of the Hittites, Amorites, Canaanites, Perizzites, Hivites and Jebusites) they came together to wage war against Joshua and Israel. However, when the people of Gibeon heard what Joshua had done to Jericho and Ai, they resorted to a ruse: They went as a delegation whose donkeys were loaded with worn-out sacks and old wineskins, cracked and mended. They put worn and patched sandals on their feet and wore old clothes. All the bread of their food supply was dry and moldy. Then they went to Joshua in the camp at Gilgal and said to him and the Israelites, "We have come from a distant country; make a treaty with us." The Israelites said to the Hivites, "But perhaps you live near us, so how can we make a treaty with you?" "We are your servants" they said to Joshua. The Israelites sampled their provisions but did not inquire of the LORD. Then*

Joshua made a treaty of peace with them to let them live, and the leaders of the assembly ratified it by oath. (Joshua 9:1-15 – NIV).

The Gibeonite spirit manifests itself in the form of craftiness, deception, trickery, lie, falsehood, shapeshifter, wolves in sheep clothing, and chameleon. These are some of the meanings of the Gibeonite Spirit. On your path to possessing your possession, you must be mindful that there are people who are masters at deception. The world is filled with deception. Even the Word of God says that the heart of man is desperately wicked, and, make no mistake, there are those who will be so jealous of you and will want to prevent you from achieving God's promises for you. Pharaoh's magicians were deceivers. They mimicked what Moses did by turning a rod into a snake when he approached them about letting the people go. However, God's power was evident when Aaron's rod swallowed up Pharaoh's magicians' snake.

The Gibeonite spirit is not genuine and can turn itself into anything to match a particular situation or scenario. So, for example, if you like grapes, all of a sudden, these people will start "liking" grapes even if they didn't at first. Or, if you have a particular interest, the spirit will pretend to have that interest. It has fake compatibility in an attempt for you to form binding contracts with them that will eventually ruin you. The ruin usually comes once they start to show their true colours. These contracts can be in the form of marriage, business deals, pregnancies, etc.

It is therefore extremely important that you seek the face of God when entering a contract with any individual. Joshua sought the Lord in almost everything he did, but he did not seek the Lord when they entered into an oath with the Gibeonites; therefore, they found themselves in a situation they could not get out of.

I declare that whoever is operating in a Gibeonite spirit in your life will receive the fire of God. They will become your slave: *"Hewers of wood and drawers of water for you."* The trick will backfire on them.

The Power Of Having The Right Self-Image: Perception

As a man thinketh in heart so is he. (see Proverbs 23:7).

God has blessed us tremendously. The universe is flowing with an abundance of resources and material blessings. This is our inheritance, but unfortunately, many will never experience the abundance because they are unable to see beyond their limitations. When we fail to see beyond our present circumstance or state, we are placed in a very dangerous situation because our mental picture is now distorted; as it is within, so it is without. How you see yourself is contributed to a number of self-impressions built up over the years, and these influence how you think and feel. The self-images can be very positive, giving a person confidence in their thoughts and actions, or they can be very negative, making a person doubtful in their capabilities. Genetics and your environment play a vital role in your perception. If you have a negative perception, whatever is placed before you will be negatively affected by your inner programming.

According to Maxwell Maltz, "The brain wants to stay in the familiar; your subconscious mind is programmed to protect itself. When it goes off course, there is a built-in mechanism in your mind that will ensure that you come back to that familiar place." Even if this thing is something that is good for you and will take you to accomplishing your vision, the fact that it is unfamiliar will cause blockage in your mind. This is the reason many people remain stuck.

We see in 1st Samuel 17 that David had a powerful perception of himself, and he knew what he was capable of. Long before anyone knew of his capabilities, he was fighting lions and bears in the field. In his mental picture, Goliath was no match. Saul was projecting doubt unto David in I Samuel 17:33 by stating, *"Thou art not able to go against this Philistine… for thou art but a youth, and he is a man of war from his youth." (KJV)*. David's image was in God and not shaken because he knew who he was being prepared to be.

In another instance in the Bible, we see the children of Israel on their final lap to enter Canaan. Moses sent men from the twelve tribes of Israel according to the command of the Lord to seek out the promised land. Numbers 13:30 says, *"Caleb came and said to Moses, let us go up at once and possess it; for we are well able to overcome it." (Number 13:30 - KJV)*. Caleb was speaking positively. However, in Numbers 13:33, the other men with him had a different image of themselves. Their report was, *"And there we saw the giants, the sons of Anak,*

100

which come of the giants: and we were in our own sight as grasshoppers, and so we were in their sight." (*KJV*).

It is observed in these instances that negative perception can be a deterrent to us possessing our possession. God has placed a desire in your heart, whether it is to start a business, go to university, move to another country, or even leave an abusive situation, but you find that there is fear in taking action.

According to Orison Marsden, "We dream a particular dream, see a particular vision because we have the talent and the special ability to bring the dream or the vision to reality." He further states that "There is a divinity behind the visions. They are prophecies of our possible future, and Holy Spirit is throwing up these pictures on our mental screen to give us a glimpse of the possibilities that are awaiting us."

It is important to note that how you see yourself will determine your outcome of either success or failure. What you see is what you get. When you create clear images of desired outcomes, there will be a divine conspiracy that will work on your behalf. Therefore, see the things you want to see and ignore that which you do not want.

- Be mindful of who you are.
- No matter how you feel, never give up.
- Offer praise.
- Meditate on the Word of God.
- The power of thought can catapult you in the right direction.
- Have the desire for the will of God.
- Know who God says you are.

The Power Of Trodding It Alone

There are instances in life that require you to trod alone on your path to possessing the possession. Understanding this is critical to the process. There are people, some well-meaning with good intentions, who can prevent you from the promise or your destiny. They can be family members, including mother, father, sister, or friends. These people have the "Crab inna barrel mentality." These people will pull you down every time you try to rise.

Remember, you would have had an awakening of who you are, and you would have sought the Lord for direction. If they are oblivious to your process, it will

102

be difficult for them to support you even if they tried because they are still operating in their old mindset. If these people are still operating with a limiting belief system, they will eventually sabotage your effort or your progress. It is very important that you pray for discernment so you know who to take or not to take along with you.

There are times when separation is very important. You may ask why? Think about this simple scenario: you have taken the decision to lose weight; you know this is vital for your health or you just want to be able to fit properly in your clothes. Imagine having a family member who has the belief that a lot of food is a way to show love. This person decides to feed you all the goodies, countering all the efforts you have put into losing the weight. In their minds, they are just showing love, but on the flip side, it is preventing you from achieving your goal. This is further compounded if you have not fully developed the strength to resist temptations.

Let's examine another scenario: the Lord commanded Abraham to pack all his possession and leave the land of Ur to the land of great possession. The Lord said, "Go into this place that I have prepared for you." (Genesis 12:1 - KJV). Abraham made the decision to follow the Lord's command. Abraham, however, took along with him his father, Terah, and his nephew, Lot. Now we know the story of the jealousy that arose with Lot, and there was a great breaking away. He ended up sharing the land with Lot, who got some of the best areas.

The Bible indicated that Abraham did not flourish until his father Terah died. There are some people who will have to die for you to possess your promise and for you to flourish. It is therefore important that you ask for discernment and not let your emotions take over when you are in the process of deciding to trod alone. Depart from their company; some of them mean you no good. Some people are destiny killers and will do everything to sabotage your effort, so be careful.

Do not take individuals with you (family or friends) who have not done the work of bettering themselves or changing their mindset. You must remember the work that was required for you to reach this phase in life. Often these people who are close to us cannot appreciate our walk and will sabotage us. They have gotten comfortable in their set ways, and it is important that you disconnect and make the trod solo.

Joseph was sold into slavery by his very own brothers. He told them he had a dream, and in it, he saw the sun and the stars bowing down to him. However, this was too much for his brothers to handle. Some will hear of your vision and conspire to eliminate you. They will also work to stop the manifestation of your destiny. We see that Joseph was placed in prison. He eventually became Governor over Egypt and Pharaoh's Chief. Joseph indirectly made the trod solo. It was not by choice, but being sold into slavery, Joseph experienced many scenarios that ultimately landed him as Chief Economist and Governor of Egypt. After many years, he could eventually say to his brothers, "…you meant evil against me, but God turned it around for my good." (Genesis 50:20 - KJV).

Not everyone is entitled to go on your destiny assignment with you. You must understand that not everyone is sincere. Not everyone can be with you during challenging times. The same individuals you thought had your back can turn on you in your vulnerability. It is therefore important that you pray for discernment and exercise wisdom as it relates to who should be with you on your journey.

The Power Of Obedience

The condition to the promise is obedience to God's law as well as following the prompting and instructions of the Holy Spirit. Setting yourself to seek the Lord should be constant practice on your journey to possessing your possession. The Bible indicates in John 10:27, *"My sheep knows my voice and another they will not follow."* (KJV). Obedience can be defined as doing what you are told to do or the ability and willingness to comply with the instructions given. It is also the process of being respectful, submissive, observant, dutiful, and yielding to order. Obedience to God's commands is the true sign of your love for God. The Bible says in Exodus 19:5, *"Now if you obey me fully and keep my covenant, then out of all nations you will be my treasured possession. Although the whole earth is mine." (KJV).*

The journey can be challenging and, at times, filled with confusion of which way to take, but by the help of the Holy Spirit, you will overcome and journey well. Obedience is greater than sacrifice. In order to excel in life, obedience to the Word of God is critical for you.

106

We see in two scenarios in the Bible where God commanded Abraham to "Get yourself and your family, go to a place that is outside your fathers land that I will show you." (see Genesis 12:1). Another time he told him, "Get your only son, Isaac, and make a sacrifice unto me." (see Genesis 22:2). In both instances, Abraham obeyed and was later called a friend of God. Obedience to God, the Father, God, the Son, and God, the Holy Spirit, will indeed make you His friend. There is power in obedience that will lead you to joy, peace, success, promotion, and the abundant life you seek, but first, you must understand that it takes time to develop. In order to get in the habit of obedience, you must acknowledge the following:

- Know that the promise is contingent on your obedience.
- You must acknowledge the promptings of the Holy Spirit.
- You must read the Word of God.
- You must believe in the power of obedience.
- You must eliminate doubt.
- You must act speedily.

If you are willing and obedient, you will eat the good of the land. According to Proverbs 22:29 – "Do you see a man that is diligent, obedient, humble, respectful and submissive in his business, work, duties, role, he will stand before kings; he will not stand before obscure men." (KJV). The scripture is packed with the principles of obedience, and we must understand that the path to possessing the promises of God is by way of obedience. By being obedient, you will stand before kings and not obscure men, and you will be favored among your peers in a strange land. In addition, you will be distinguished in everything you do.

Are you following the direction that God is commanding you to go? Are you moving towards the prompting of the Holy Spirit? If you feel like you are confused on the path to your destiny, it could be that you are not obedient to God's instructions. Set time to seek the Lord and asked Him to help you follow His instructions.

The Power Of Being In The Right Place

I have observed something else under the sun. The fastest runner doesn't always win the race, and the strongest warrior doesn't always win the

battle. The wise sometimes go hungry, and the skillful are not necessarily wealthy. And those who are educated don't always lead successful lives. It is all decided by chance, by being in the right place at the right time. (Ecclesiastes 9:11 – NLT).

Being in the right place is God-appointed. There are times in your life when you might have a prompting to go to a particular location, and suddenly something unforgettable or miraculous happens that you did not anticipate or plan for. This thing that happened could have only occurred at that particular place. Rest assured, there is a place that is awaiting you with your miracle and provision. If God has given you the vision, then He will make the provision. But also know this, being in the right place at the right time does not necessarily mean being in a physical place; there is a spiritual condition that is required, and it pertains to your heart.

The Bible warns us that "The heart is deceitful above all things, and desperately wicked; who can know it?" (Jeremiah 17:9 - NKJV), which is why it also teaches us, "Keep thy heart with all diligence; for out of it are the issues of life." (Proverbs 4:23 – KJV). Another translation says, "Keep your heart with all diligence, for out of it spring the issues of life." (NKJV). It is therefore important for us to have the right heart posture, which is focused on what God wants, and we should obey His commands. With your hearts in the right place, God can begin to work miracles that are beyond your human comprehension.

Now, as it relates to physical places, we see holy places and altars that stand as monuments of the Lord's faithfulness to His people throughout the Bible. These were real places with powerful reminders of real events that had taken place there. God has a blessing for you, but that blessing is tied to a particular location. In order for us to tap into this place, we need to let the Holy Spirit be our GPS. When the Holy Spirit is our GPS, He will lead us to where God is working and where we will get our breakthrough.

So many biblical figures were required to be in a particular place for spectacular things to happen. David was required to be in the field tending to the sheep where he gained the skills required to kill lions and bears, which would have prepared him for his ultimate opponent Goliath. Joseph was required to be in the place of prison to interpret a dream that would

110

later bring him to the King's palace, interpreting dreams that ultimately landed him a role as Governor over all of Egypt. Abraham was required to leave one place called Ur of the Chaldean and go to another place called Canaan, where he was blessed immensely.

Ruth from Moab, who was married to Naomi's son, decided to tarry with Naomi even in the midst of impossibility. Ruth went back to Naomi's hometown of Bethlehem, and at that time, the harvesters were reaping barley. Naomi sent Ruth out to glean barley behind the harvesters as this was how poor people survived. It just so happened that the field where Ruth went to glean belonged to one of Naomi's relatives, a wonderful man named Boaz. He began to pay attention to Ruth and told his harvesters to leave a little more behind than normal so she would have plenty of grain to take home. Ruth received favor; she was in the right place at the right time.

The Bible says, *"Naomi her mother-in-law said to her, "My daughter, I need to seek some security for you, so that it may be well with you. Now here is our kinsman Boaz, with whose young women you have been working. See, he is winnowing barley tonight at the threshing floor. Now wash and anoint yourself, and put on your best clothes and go down to the threshing floor; but do not make yourself known to the man until he has finished eating and drinking. When he lies down, observe the place where he lies; then, go and uncover his feet and lie down; and he will tell you what to do." She said to her, "All that you tell me I will do.""* (Ruth 3:1-5 – NIV).

Now Boaz was an honorable man. He married Ruth, and they built a life together which received the blessings of God. This union produced a great and mighty King. The Bible says, *"So Boaz took Ruth and she became his wife. When he made love to her, the Lord enabled her to conceive, and she gave birth to a son. The women said to Naomi: "Praise be to the Lord, who this day has not left you without a guardian-redeemer. May he become famous throughout Israel! He will renew your life and sustain you in your old age. For your daughter-in-law, who loves you and who is better to you than seven sons, has given him birth." Then Naomi took the child in her arms and cared for him. The women living there said, "Naomi has a son!" And they named him Obed. He was the father of Jesse, the father of David."* (Ruth 4:13-17 – NIV).

The story of Ruth demonstrates what can happen when you take the risk to be at the right place at the right time. Ruth gave up everything: her way of life, her god, and wholeheartedly accepted Naomi as her family. She took the chance and went with Naomi to Bethlehem. That chance allowed her to find favour with Boaz, and it changed the trajectory of her life. Are you at the right place? Is your heart in the right place? Pray and ask God, the Father, to help you to be in the right place. Follow the prompting of the Holy Spirit GPS and you will find your right place, the place that will lead you to destiny.

Important to note is that your "right place" may not look or feel like you want it in the initial stage. When you get to your place, you shouldn't expect your assignment to necessarily be easy straight away. Your right place comes with challenges! It may be tough for a moment. You might even feel like giving up and returning to your familiar comfort zone. The challenges can even make you question whether you heard God correctly. But rest assured that His strength is made perfect in our weakness even with the challenges that we face.

Abraham faced many difficulties on his journey. Even though he was given a promise, his journey did not look that promising to begin with. At one point, he even left the Promised Land and went down to Egypt, where he faced a high degree of vulnerability. He feared his wife being taken by the King because of her beauty. He even feared for his life. His decision brought destruction and plague upon the King of Egypt. Could he have done things differently? Did the father of faith lose faith in times of hardship? Did he not believe God could have provided another way out? These are questions we need to ask as we navigate the challenges that might occur in our "right place." Do not let a difficult situation force you out of your right place. You might be in your right place in many areas of your life; it could be on your path to pursuing higher education and you cannot find the school fees. It might be your marriage that is shaking; your house might be up for repossession. Trust and extend your faith. Whatever the challenges you are facing today, do not let it move you out of your right place. Once God has led you and has given you the promise, hold on and He will make the way that will lead you to the right people and open doors that can bless you tremendously. Stay in your right place!

The Power Of Being Intentional

Look carefully then how you walk, not as unwise but as wise, making the best use of the time, because the days are evil. Therefore do not be foolish, but understand what the will of the Lord is. (Ephesians 5:15-17 – ESV).

The pressures of everyday living can have you in a tailspin, and it can get even more complicated on your path to achieving what God has set out for you. Distractions from people and things can steal your time, leaving you with a feeling of emptiness. To combat distractions, you must be intentional about achieving the goals you set. Think back to a time when you decided to go after or take action on that thing that was impressed upon your heart. It might have been a new discovery, new hobby, or even a new book. At the time, you were certain that this was right for you, and you even made a mental commitment to continue on the path. But as you look back now, you realize that much of that knowledge is not operating in your life. Where did it go? Have you followed through on your commitment to exercise or learn that second language? Are you continuing on the path to self-discovery? Our lives can get very busy with the everyday mundane things that will slowly eat away our time.

When we are developing a new habit or have taken the decision to make a life-changing impact, we can easily follow the path of least resistance and get sidetracked. It is therefore necessary that you become intentional in achieving your goals. Being intentional means getting clear upfront about what you want to achieve. You intentionally set an intention to achieve your vision and the specific goals that are important to you. John Maxwell quote: "If I wanted to make a difference…Wishing for things to change wouldn't make them change. Hoping for improvements wouldn't bring them. Dreaming wouldn't provide all the answers I needed. Vision wouldn't be enough to bring transformation to me or others. Only by managing my thinking and shifting my thoughts from desire to deeds would I be able to bring about positive change. I needed to go from wanting to doing." We must be intentional about taking action while we are in the process.

We have discussed in the first section on getting clear on the will of God for your life as well as the importance of prayer and journaling time. These are a significant part of the process of being intentional.

116

You need to carve out time and be intentional in order to build momentum towards your vision. The Bible says in James 2:26, "For as the body without the spirit is dead, so faith without works is dead also." (NKJV). Wishful thinking will not get you to your vision. Being deliberate by setting aside time and resources will ultimately lead to where God is calling you. Have you been intentional about achieving your goals? Are you intentional about setting time to seek God? Make the commitment today; it will surely lead to the right path.

The Power Of Deliverance

In order for you to step into your wealthy place, there must be deliverance. According to Obadiah 17, the first step to possessing your possession is deliverance. Obadiah wrote, *"But upon Mount Zion shall be deliverance, and there shall be holiness, and the house of Jacob shall possess their possessions." (Obadiah 1:17 - KJV).*

To deliver is to save from something or someone. It is to be free from bondage or yoke. It is to be disconnected from every wrong connection, association, covenant, and power. One of the greatest deliverances was with the children of Israel coming out of Egyptian bondage. It shows the mighty power of God, who is the Author and Finisher of our faith. In order for the Israelites to enter into the promised land, there needed to be deliverance.

In order for you to possess your possession, you need deliverance. You need to be free from all the yokes and bondages that tell you that you cannot make it, you are not good enough, you are not qualified enough, or you are not worthy enough. You have an inheritance as a child of God, and because of this, you are true owners of all good things in life. It is for you to know the truth and walk in that truth of who God has called you to be. It is a birthright that comes with your new life in Christ, and it has given you the right to own and enjoy everything that belongs to God, your Father.

To gain an understanding of the limitless possessions within your reach as a child of God, the best angle is to consider the majestic power, wisdom, glory, dominion, and riches of almighty God. God's possessions and riches have no limits, no boundaries, no beginning, and no end. As God's children, nothing less is expected of you because you are a partaker of His divine nature and grace. The scripture says in 2 Peter 1:3, "According as his divine power

118

hath given unto us all things that pertain unto life and godliness, through the knowledge of him that hath called us to glory and virtue." (KJV). With this declaration, it is clear that God has already given you all things required to possess your possessions. However, considering the situation of many of God's children, it is extremely sad to see a majority living like servants, as though they own nothing, whereas God's Word says all things belong to them.

It is absolutely true that all things have been given to you as God's child, but it is critical you understand how to possess those things which God has freely given to you as an inheritance. Otherwise, there is no way you will enjoy or live the life expected of you. To take actual possession of the land, the children of Israel firmly stood their ground, fought, and claimed that which God had declared to be their inheritance by prevailing against and displacing the Canaanites. You also can have all good things in life, which God says are your inheritance, as long as you are prepared to take the practical steps to possess them. Many times, the things blocking us are our own minds and limitations that we have due to a lack faith and understanding who we are. There are also times when the yoke is brought about by others who are adamant about blocking our progress and preventing us from reaching our purpose.

God said to Moses, "I am the LORD. I appeared to Abraham, to Isaac and to Jacob as God Almighty, but by my name the LORD. I did not make myself fully known to them. I also established my covenant with them to give them the land of Canaan, where they resided as foreigners. Moreover, I have heard the groaning of the Israelites, whom the Egyptians are enslaving, and I have remembered my covenant.

"Therefore, say to the Israelites: 'I am the LORD, and I will bring you out from under the yoke of the Egyptians. I will free you from being slaves to them, and I will redeem you with an outstretched arm and with mighty acts of judgment. I will take you as my own people, and I will be your God. Then you will know that I am the LORD your God, who brought you out from under the yoke of the Egyptians. And I will bring you to the land I swore with uplifted hand to give to Abraham, to Isaac and to Jacob. I will give it to you as a possession. I am the LORD.'" (Exodus 6:9 - NIV).

The Lord moved mightily to deliver His people out of the hands of the Egyptians, and He will do the

120

same for you, but there are times when you must take steps that are within your reach to allow you to reach purpose. There might be issues, such as deep-rooted trauma, that are blocking your progress, and this might require that you receive the required help from professionals who can help you navigate to the next level. The Holy Spirit can help in this area as long as you confess and ask for help with those issues you might not be aware of. Pray that the Holy Spirit will bring back to your remembrance all the hidden things you need to be healed of in your life. In order to possess your possession, the following might be some of the things you need deliverance from:

- Ignorance: The greatest deliverance is that of ignorance. The Bible says people are destroyed because of a lack of knowledge (see Hosea 4:6).

- Evil binding covenants, whether inherited or personally entered into.

- Sickness and diseases.

- Demonic bondage.

- Sin.

- Trauma and deep-rooted issues.

Deliverance is the path to freedom and possession. It is through deliverance you manifest the vision that God has given you. When a man is delivered, he can now settle down to live for God and possess his inheritance.

All ties with the devil must be cut for one to possess his inheritance in Christ. Do you perceive that you might need deliverance from the abovementioned issues? If so, you should consider seeking the required help. You can also repent, renounce, and reject sin and turn from ways that are not pleasing to God. He promised that if my people who are called by my name should humble themselves and pray and turn from their wicked ways, then He will hear from heaven and heal their land (see 2 Chronicles 7:14). He can bring healing to you and me so we can step into our possession.

The Power Of Waging A Good Warfare Over Your Stuff

It is your responsibility to partner with God when He makes you a promise.

A vision from God is like an announcement of His intention for your life. So it is with a prophetic word that is spoken out of the mouth of His servants. However, not because you have seen the vision and received the word means that it will automatically come to pass. There are times when there is a war against you from the enemy's camp because of your prophetic word. You may encounter warfare because the enemy has seen your star and has an inclination that you are created for greatness. Because of this, you may encounter great challenges on your path to your possession.

Moses was born to be a great deliverer for the children of Israel, but right after he was born, a decree was sent out for the destruction of all the male children. His mother had to disguise him in a basket, after which Pharoah's daughter found him, which allowed him to be saved and ultimately deliver the children of Israel as he moved into adulthood. We also see where wise men saw the star of baby Jesus and communicated to King Herod that a child was born who is King of the Jews. Mary and Joseph had to flee Bethlehem after the birth of Jesus so that His destiny would not be aborted by the king's decree to kill all male children during that time.

Just as in these scenarios with Moses and Jesus Christ, so it is at times with your vision and prophetic words. The enemy saw the birthing of where you are headed in life and wants to kill it before it manifests. It is your responsibility to partner with God so your vision will manifest in the natural. It is your responsibility to wage a good warfare by praying, staying in the Word, listening, and obeying the instructions from God. Paul instructed Timothy that he should wage a good warfare over the words that were given to him (see 1 Timothy 1:18). It was important because the prophecies helped Timothy focus his life and ministry according to the call of God. Paul charged Timothy as he wrote, *"This charge I commit to you, son Timothy, according to the prophecies previously made concerning you, that by them you may wage the good warfare." (1 Timothy 1:18 - NKJV)*. It means to be active about it, staying on course, and having the right conscience to guide you. It is the enemy's plan to weary you and cause you to lose focus, but a part of waging war is actively pursuing the visions and goals God has given to you as well as praying over your prophetic words.

As you partner with God, know that *"God is watching over His words and promises to perform*

124

it." (Jeremiah 1:12 – ESV). You must believe that there will be a great performance that will transform your life, but you must execute war. Here are some strategies to wage a good warfare:

- Pray over your vision, goals, and prophetic words.
- Stay in the Word of God.
- Listen to the prompting of the Holy Spirit.
- Follow instructions by taking action.

"Elijah was a man just like us. He prayed earnestly that it would not rain, and it did not rain on the land for three and a half years. Again he prayed, and the heavens gave rain, and the earth produced its crops." (James 5:17-18 – BSB).

I encourage you to pray and birth your vision as you journey on the path to possessing your possession, and as you engage in war, do not get weary in well doing.

PHASE 4:

UNDERSTANDING AND NAVIGATING CHALLENGES/DELAYS ON THE JOURNEY

The Enemy And Your Possession

The Bible reminds us in John 10:10 *"The thief cometh to kill steal and destroy: but I am come that you might have life and have it more abundantly." (KJV).* There is an invisible thief that we cannot see with a mandate to kill, steal, and destroy that which God has ordained for us. There is a spiritual battle that we face in light of us possessing our possession. This battle or war is invisible. It is in the invisible realm that we cannot see with our natural eye, and it is therefore important that we ask God to open our eyes to see in the unseen.

"For we wrestle not against flesh and blood, but against principalities, against powers, against the rulers of the darkness of this world, against spiritual wickedness in high places." (Ephesians 6:12 - KJV).

In another translation, the phrase "not against flesh and blood" is translated to say we are not fighting against people made of flesh and blood. In other words, we are not merely fighting against the people who are around us and who hurt us.

We are not only struggling with our egos and our little selfish desires; the Bible says we are fighting against the spiritual forces of evil in the heavenly places. We see this translated in 2 Kings 6:15-19. The great prophet, Elisha, had spiritual eyesight, so he was able to help the king of Israel avoid any traps that the enemy, the king of Aram, had set up. Later, King Aram found that Elisha was the one disrupting all his plans. He was furious and sent his whole army to capture the prophet. When Elisha's servant saw the troops of the enemy marching towards the people of Israel, he was so afraid. Elisha said to his servant, "Fear not: for they that be with us are more than they that be with them" (2 Kings 6:16 - KJV) and prayed for him. When the Lord opened the servant's eyes, and when he looked up to the hillside, he saw many of God's mighty armies protecting him and his master from the enemy.

Like Elisha, we need to ask God to open our eyes in the spirit to perceive the invisible realities, in particular, the authenticity of God's mighty heavenly angels. They are fighting for us during our challenging times. With this knowledge, as you move into your possession, ask the Lord to open your spiritual eyes so you know you stand protected on the journey to what God has ordained for you. It is important for you to remember that you are battling from the standpoint of victory; you are already victorious, and the battle is already won.

When Jehoshaphat battled an army in 2 Chronicles 20, the Lord spoke and told him that the battle was the Lord's, and Jehoshaphat won the war against Judah. He heeded the Word of the Lord; he spoiled the enemy, and he and his people entered into great rest. I declare over you that there will be a divine ambushment over your enemies, and you will possess your possession and enter into great rest.

The Spirit Of Delay

Dealing with delay is another important element that you must understand in order for you to possess your possession. Delay means to put something off or postpone until later or to cause something to take longer or to be late. Understanding this element in actualizing God's promise is vital for your possession. I will explore three situations/reasons that may cause a delay.

Analysis Of Biblical Delays

There are instances of delayed manifestation; this happens when things are seen in the spirit but refuse to manifest in reality. Additionally, there is also delayed expectation. You expect an event, but all forces seem to be working against you to prevent manifestation from happening. There are also cases of delay in prophetic fulfillment, and this can be illustrated by the story of Joseph. Joseph knew the sun and the moon would bow down to him, but he was still in prison. After thirty years, he saw his dream come to pass. Have you ever encountered such a type of delay, where the prophetic word was spoken? You have seen the vision, but it seems as though it is not forthcoming?

Being foolish can cause a delay of our destiny. Using the example of the ten virgins in Matthew 25, we see the case of the five wise who had oil in their lamps and the five foolish who were playing around and did not get any oil until the appointed time. When they eventually left to get oil, the bridegroom came, and the door was shut preventing them from entering by the time they got back. Have you waited too long to do something you know you should have done and refused to do it? That waiting or procrastinating could be the cause of your delay in the promise. Being unequally yoked is also another cause for the blessing being delayed. Amos 3:3 says two cannot walk unless they agree. Therefore, if you are not in

131

agreement with where you desire to go, or even if you are not in agreement with your spouse, it causes one to go deeper into bondage and make it even more difficult to escape delays.

Delayed By God Or Delayed By The Process

There are instances when God's timing does not seem to align with our timing, and we feel that what is promised to us is taking much longer than it should. I must highlight to you that being outside the will of God may be a critical factor, and we must learn to trust God's timing. On the journey to our promise, we must remember that "...he who began a good work in you will carry it on to completion..." (Philippians 1:6 – NIV). If we want God's will for our lives, we need to learn to wait. Patience is key because the vision is for an appointed time, and though it may take a long time, we are encouraged to wait for it.

God sets out a timeline for His promises to come to pass. How we understand, yield or cooperate with this dynamic brings us closer to God's perfect will. The children of Israel wandered in the wilderness for forty years, yet Joshua's men spied out the promised

132

land in forty days. What was the difference between these scenarios?

It is vital that we realize that not every delay is demonically designed. We see the scenario with Joseph who was sold into slavery by his brothers. He spent many years in captivity, but his journey was meant for a great deliverance. There are instances in our lives when it seems as though the journey is the plan of the enemy. Why is this so? The trauma, pain, loss, smear, lies, suffering—one might ask, "Why would God allow these events in my life?" This is where it takes deep discernment and an understanding that what seems like it is meant for bad is divinely intended for our good, growth, and the glory of God.

Therefore, understanding the element of time and the will of God is important on your journey to possessing your possession. Habakkuk 2:3 highlights, "This vision is for a future time. It describes the end, and it will be fulfilled. If it seems slow in coming, wait patiently, for it will surely take place. It will not be delayed." While we wait on God, we are encouraged to find out what it is that God is waiting on us for. Many times we are delayed because God is waiting on us to carry out our end of the bargain. When I made the covenant with Lord, I promised that if God opened the doors for me to go to university, then I would serve Him. He did open many doors in the form of scholarships in bachelor's and master's degrees, plus numerous certifications. I have never spent one dollar to receive my education. God opened supernatural doors at all times for me, but did I honor my side of the agreement? Not immediately; it took me years to do the work of God. I realized I was delayed, and at one point, I was stuck. It was then He called out to me in a loud voice and said, "Tracey, the promise!" He reminded me of my side of the covenant. It was after that encounter that I moved speedily to work in the vineyard for the Lord. I encourage you to examine yourself and see what God is waiting on you for.

Delayed For Self-Development

Another reason we might be delayed is due to our own self. We might be the one standing in the way of our own progress. We should ask the question, "While I wait on God, what is it that God is waiting on me for?" In many instances, we are required to match the promise God has for us, and this is where we might be delayed, for maturity and character building. Think about a high-powered weapon in the hands of a child; one thing that comes to my mind is mass destruction. So it is with God's promises. The magnitude of the promise might be very great, and in order for you to be successful, maturity and character building are required.

David was on the farm fighting lions and bear in preparation to meet the Philistine Goliath of Goth. It took David approximately thirty years from the time he was anointed by the prophet Samuel before he actually became King. During the years of waiting, David was being trained because his future role was mighty. If your promise is that you are going to be in a position to have great financial blessings, then it will be required of you to be able to manage your finances.

If you are currently at a point where you are weak in that area, then the Holy Spirit will prompt you in the areas that you require development and maturity. That is the reason I highlight that our own selves may be the cause of our own delay.

Another scenario is that the Holy Spirit might have instructed us to take a specific action which is crucial for the next step for the victory, and we delay in taking that step. It may be due to fear, procrastination, and not having the right self-image of who God says we are. This is where it is key for you to analyze your own self to see what God is waiting on you to get rid of. It is important that you do not fall prey to the trap of procrastination and laziness. One of the roles of the Holy Spirit is to guide you in all truth about yourselves. You can delay yourself when you fail to yield to the prompting of the Spirit of God and do the developmental work that is necessary for you to possess your possession. I encourage you, yield to Holy Spirit, and He will counsel and teach you.

Satanic/Demonic Delay

Another element of delay on the path to possessing your possession is through demonic networking. There are times when we are being delayed because of satan and his demonic networking. The Bible indicates that Daniel prayed for the destiny of Israel to change. The Lord said from the first time Daniel prayed, his prayers were answered. However, the prince of the kingdom of Persia withstood him for twenty-one days and, had it not been for Michael, one of the chief princes, the Prince of Persia would have taken charge and delayed the destiny of Israel.

There are times when your prayers are in the will of God, and the answer is already given, but the enemy steps in to delay your progress. You must be mindful that the enemy is very strategic, and the delay is caused to remove you out of the timing of God's blessings. It will also make you question God and can prompt you to take matters into your own hands and lead to the scenario of hope being deferred which makes the heart sick (see Proverbs 13:12). When the heart is sick, it leaves an open door for demonic occurrence such as disappointment, deception, discouragement, depression, and anger.

It is very important that you learn to identify these traps of the enemy and reject and renounce his plot by getting your heart healed. The demonic networking thrives in a wounded and sick heart and therefore deliverance from these strongholds is critical for you to walk in the promises ordained for you. Becoming familiar with this understanding can prevent many would-be delays.

As we walk towards our promises, we should do an analysis of the incidences that occurred in our lives and see where there are signs of demonic entity. This will help us identify whether the delay was God-ordained or demonically assigned. Psalm 121 says

137

the sun will not smite you by day or the moon by night. The enemy can use the elements of this earth to trap, stop and delay you, but you must declare that the sun will not smite you by day nor the moon by night. Declare that any evil programming against your destiny must be nullified in the name of Jesus Christ of Nazareth.

When Joshua fought the battle at Jericho, he commanded the sun to stand still (see Joshua 10:13). Please know that you have the power to command the elements to work for you. Jericho was shut; nothing was going in and out. The sorcerers, diviners, and soothsayers who sent arrows by day began to panic when Joshua commanded the sun to stand still. The diviners were using the power of the sun. Joshua spoke to God and said, "I cannot fight this battle while the sun is still moving," so Joshua commanded in agreement with almighty God and got the victory. I declare that the sun will not go down with your victory in Jesus' Name; not you, not your household. In the name of Jesus, the sun will not go down with your breakthrough.

Lingering At The Place Of Refreshing

The Challenge Of "Almost-There-But-Never-There": The Spirit Of Kadesh Barnea

Can you remember a time when you have seen or tasted that thing you were absolutely sure you would possess, occupy or dominate? There are times in your journey that you might miss the breakthrough to the promised land. The challenge of almost-there-but-never-making-it-in is so real for many of us. You were so sure of manifestation, and then something happened; something happened that prevented you from putting your foot on that land or in that house or at that job or even in that university.

It could have even prevented you from finishing that job and taking the step into your purpose. You begin to question yourself because you were so sure that thing was yours. You have dreamt about it and made all the necessary preparations for it. You were at the edge of just crossing over. You looked and you saw it steering back at you. It was sure, but you never manifested it. This scenario, I can tell you, have such a gut-wrenching feeling of frustration and failure. You asked yourself the question, "How could this be?" You might even ask God what is happening.

139

You are now second guessing yourself. The spirit of almost-there-but-never-there is operating in your life. I call it the spirit of Kadesh Barnea. This spirit can manifest itself in your life in the following way: it can be synonymous with being in the wrong position where expectations and hope are always dashed. With this spirit, failure becomes present on the day of favor; you go around in circles without much progress. You are being singled out for blackmail or blacklisted punishment; your name is forgotten (for example, for an interview or special purposes). You might even see repeated patterns of rejection, coming back to square one with nothing to show. Your destiny helpers are becoming hateful and uncooperative. You experience failure at the edge of your breakthroughs, and disappointments become the norm.

In Deuteronomy 2, the Lord announces to Moses that it was now time for the people to move and take possession of the promised land. Moses was now of old age; he understood the wisdom and fury of God. He arose and stood on the hill overlooking River Jordan and the great promised land that he would only see from a distance but never possess. He must have thought to himself, "Is there even a slim chance of me making it in? After all, I have done all the work

140

to journey on to this point. Is there the slightest possibility?" Sadly, that would not be.

As Moses recounted the journey to the point of possession, he spoke to the people and reminded them of their rebellious nature during the wilderness. It was their fault why he would not taste of this goodness. Moses prayed to the Lord in Deuteronomy 3:24-27, *"O Lord God, You have begun to show Your servant Your greatness and Your mighty hand, for what god is there in heaven or on earth who can do anything like Your works and Your mighty deeds? I pray, let me cross over and see the good land beyond the Jordan, those pleasant mountains, and Lebanon."*

"But the Lord was angry with me on your account, and would not listen to me. So the Lord said to me: 'Enough of that! Speak no more to me of this matter. Go up to the top of Pisgah, and lift your eyes toward the west, the north, the south, and the east; behold it with your eyes, for you shall not cross over this Jordan." (KJV)).

Those words were sharp and piercing and must have wounded Moses' heart to know that he could only see but would never enter the promised land. The

141

incidences that led to this happened at a place called Kadesh-Barnea. Kadesh-Barnea was situated on the border between Canaan, the promised land, and the sandy stretches of the desert through which the children of Israel had traversed after leaving Egypt. God's original intention was that this place would have been symbolic for a short stop that would only be eleven days in. It should have been a place to regroup and refresh before ultimately taking over the promised land, but through disobedience and unbelief, the people of God made it a destination. Influenced by the discouraging negative reports, the people abandoned all hope of entering the promised land. They remained a considerable time at Kadesh-Barnea and, because of their unbelief, they were condemned by God to wander for thirty-eight years in the wilderness.

God planned that Kadesh-Barnea should be a gateway through which His chosen people would march to obtain their inheritance. Instead, it became a dwelling place where a lack of faith and rebellion caused the people of God to spend forty years wandering in the wilderness. Many died in this place: the grandparents and great grandparents did not make it into the promised land; only Joshua and

Caleb from that generation tasted and saw what the Lord intended for them.

Are you losing faith on the journey to your promise? Are you so overwhelmed that you have fallen into complaint and rebellion? Are you looking to go back to Egypt, the place of bondage where God has delivered you from? It could be old habits, relationships, or even a way of thinking. Is the burden to your destiny too hard to bear that you have fallen into a negative mindset? Beware! This could be the trap of the enemy at the edge of your breakthrough. Do not give up or throw in the towel. Press towards the mark. You are almost there! Strengthen yourself in the Word of God. Pray for your eyes to be opened. Ask God to deliver you on the journey so the spirit of Kadesh-Barnea does not overtake you.

Prayer Against the Spirit Of Almost-There-But-Never-There

I decree and declare that the bondage of Kadesh-Barnea be broken off your life, in the name of Jesus. Every cycle of stagnancy, I nullify you today, in the name of Jesus. Every stagnation stronghold binding you with stagnancy be removed by fire, in the name of Jesus. Every power of failure, frustration,

143

retrogression, and backwardness, be roasted by fire, in the name of Jesus Christ.

I pray the Lord give you divine power to find your bearing in the journey of life. Let every desert arrow fired into your destiny backfire to sender now, in the name of Jesus. I pray you shall get to your divine destiny at the appointed time, in the name of Jesus.

PHASE 5:

THE WAY FORWARD
THE FORMULA TO DOMINATE AND
MAINTAIN THE BLESSED LIFE

Obey the Lord your God so that all these blessings will come and stay with you: (Deuteronomy 28:2 - NCV)

I would like to encourage you that as you obey the commands of the Lord and take the bold action step of faith, you will see that all of heaven will come together to assist you. You can be a co-creator with God and step into the blessings and promises that He has ordained for you from before the foundations of the world. Ephesians 1:3 says we should praise God *"who has blessed us in the heavenly realms with every spiritual blessing in Christ."* (NIV). You will recognize on your journey that there are times when you will experience instant manifestation by the miraculous hand of God where you did not even need to intervene. These are special instances where God needs you to see His power working through you to give you faith for the journey ahead of you. Usually when this happens, there is a special call or assignment on your life. However, the majority of times require that you follow the path of God's commands, and it is on a matter of condition. This means that before we see the blessings, we must follow what God says. You must take action and get up and go after the vision, desires and goals; you have to put in some work. You must take that walk;

146

the soul of your feet must trod upon the land. Your action is required for you to step into your possession.

Moses in Deuteronomy wrote that *"All these blessings will come up on you and accompany you if you obey the Lord your God." (Deuteronomy 28:2 - NIV)*. We see the operative word is "if", which means it is conditional. So you need to analyze yourself; ask yourself, "Am I obeying the commands of God? Am I following His instructions given to me by reading the Word or through divine promptings?" Many times we expect blessings without putting in the work, and faith without action is dead and will not profit us anything. So let us maintain our possessions by implementing the following strategies:

1. Taking bold action steps of faith.

As I have said so many times, taking bold action steps of faith is what will propel you into destiny. I encourage you to follow the commands of God and be a co-creator in realizing your God-given vision, dreams, and desires. Get up and go! Faith without works is dead!

147

2. **Thanksgiving and praise: There is power in your praise. Those who have more will be given and those who have not even that which they have will be taken away (see Matthew 13:12).**

As you continue on the path to possessing your possession, one component to help you maintain the trajectory of success is thanksgiving. Having a posture of gratitude and thanksgiving opens the heavens for you to reach your next level. It is the will of God for each of us to have an attitude of gratitude. We can see this in the Bible where Paul wrote: "In everything give thanks; for this is God's will for you in Christ Jesus." (1 Thessalonians 5:18 – NKJV). When we give thanks, we build relationship with God, and it reminds us of what we have instead of what we do not have.

A heart of thanksgiving can literally alter your perspective to see the glass half-full instead of half-empty. Thanksgiving to God will keep our hearts in right relationship with Him and will save you from negative attitudes that can rob you of the peace that God wants you to experience as you pursue your visions, goals, and desires.

148

3. Continuously improve yourself, and read/meditate on the Word.

In the first chapter, I mentioned carving out time to read the Word as you try to understand the will of God for your life. But staying in the Word of God is also very important as you journey on the path to success. God told Joshua as he was leading the children of Israel to possess the promised land that this book of the law should not depart from him. The Word of God is packed with strategies and the knowledge you need to maintain everything God has given to you. David also highlighted the point about the sweetness of God's Word by saying: "*How sweet are your words to my taste! Yes, sweeter than honey to my mouth! (Psalm 119:103 – KJV).* The Word of God is the source of true wisdom and can guide you through every area of your life as you possess your possession.

When the prophet Ezekiel ate the scroll of the Word of God, he said, *"It was sweet as honey in my mouth" (Ezekiel 3:3 – NIV).* Let the sweetness of the Word be your guide. Let the Word be a lamp to guide your feet and a light to guide your path as you make the trod. By letting the Word be your guide, not only will you remember the Lord in all you do, but you will maintain your success.

4. Pray without ceasing.

We have explored the power of prayer in the first chapter. We realize that prayer is key as we maintain the trajectory to possess our possession. When we communicate with God through prayer, we get divine instructions on how to tap into the heart and mind of God. The Bible encourages us to "pray in the Spirit on all occasions with all kinds of prayers and requests." (Ephesians 6:18 – NIV).

In addition, we should not be anxious about anything, but in everything, by prayer and petition, with thanksgiving, present our requests to God (see Philippians 4:6). Through prayer, we gain an experience to build our faith with God on an emotional level. God has established prayer as part of His plan to accomplish His will through us. Therefore, on the path to possessing all God has for you, remember that prayer can clear human obstacles out of the way in order for God to work on your behalf.

5. Confession of the Word over every circumstance and being mindful of who you are, no matter how much you feel like giving up.

Affirming who you are in Christ and who He has called you to be is important. On your journey, you will experience obstacles, challenges and sometimes, you may even question if you are on the right path. It is very important that you do not lose sight of the prize. One such way is to affirm who you are. The Lord encouraged Joshua to be strong and courageous as he led the children of Israel into the promised land. They were coming up against giants and needed to be reminded of who they were. So it is with you as you walk in all that God has for you.

Never lose sight of who you are, no matter how you feel. Never give up on the promise. Many start the journey well and get distracted by challenges and oppositions. Get in the Word of God and write out scriptures that are in line with your circumstances, and affirm them daily. You will be amazed how speaking the Word of God to yourself can transform your circumstances. You should be mindful that the battle is already won, and He who has begun a good work in you will ensure that it is completed (see

151

Philippian 1:6). You are already victorious, so go and possess all that God has for you.

God Bless You.

A PRAYER FOR YOUR JOURNEY

Before Joshua went in to possess the promise, the Lord commanded him to "be strong and courageous" and move without fear. The Spirit of the Lord is speaking to you today, and He is saying, "Fear not, for I am with you always."

I pray that all your heart's desires will come to pass. I pray that you will manifest your most cherished dreams and visions. I pray that you walk in the knowledge that you are divinely protected. I pray that you become intimate with God as your source. I pray that the flood gates of heaven will shower down your blessings and give you witty inventions and strategies to possess your possessions.

It is well with you and with the works of your hands.

God bless you!

Peace!

A CALL FOR YOUR SALVATION

If you are reading this book and you are not yet a child of God, I encourage you to accept Jesus Christ as your Lord and Saviour by confessing your sins in sincere repentance and forsaking them. Ask God to cleanse you of all unrighteousness and forgive you of your sins. Ask Him to come into your heart and dwell there and make you His own. Then ask the Holy Spirit to baptize you with fire and power like on the day of Pentecost (see Act 2).

Commit to a life of Christian living in total dedication to God in obedience and holiness. Feed on the Word daily by reading your Bible and be prayerful always.

ABOUT THE AUTHOR

 Tracey-Ann Wright is an Author, Policy Writer, and International Development Consultant with 15+ years of professional experience moving fluidly through finance, agriculture, and policy development. She has been involved in national and regional development as a Consultant to the Agricultural Sector, Banker, Agricultural Economist, Policy Analyst, and Researcher. Previously, Tracey-Ann worked in the Government of Jamaica and the United Nations, where she has contributed to the development of numerous agricultural investment policies and strategies. Throughout her career, she has developed, organized, and led Trade Missions for the United Nations, International Trade Center, Agricultural Sector Strategy, and represented the Government of Jamaica in policy dialogue in continents such as

Europe, Asia, North America, Latin America, and the Caribbean.

Tracey-Ann holds a Master of Science degree (MSc.) in Agricultural Entrepreneurship from the University of the West Indies (Mona) and a Bachelor of Business Administration Degree (Hons) in Finance and International Business from the University of Technology Jamaica. While at University, she was the recipient of the University of Technology Foundation Scholarship and contributed to student development as an Executive Student Council leader.

One of Tracey-Ann's passions is to create development opportunities to assist vulnerable women and youth create positive change. She currently serves as Board of Director and Deputy Program Development Director to the United Nations Association in Canada, Calgary Branch. She also served as Youth Director in her local Ministry in Jamaica, where she assisted vulnerable youths by providing mentorship in the areas of finance and goal settings to better improve their lives.

She has experienced supernatural encounters with the Holy Spirit that has led to her great deliverance and healing, and has seen the power of God being made manifest in her own terminally ill relative who was taken off life support to the doctor's amazement after her prayers and intercession.

Tracey-Ann has purposed to help individuals in the body of Christ to step in their God-given calling by using biblical, transformative principles and is a firm believer that true evidence of the Kingdom of God is to make the sick well, the poor rich and the weak strong.

REFERENCE

1. Edmunson, Ron (2015), *7 Ways to Distinguish God's Voice from the Circumstances of Life:*
2. https://missionbibleclass.org/old-testament/part1/conquering-the-land/the-gibeonite-trick/
3. https://www.smartsheet.com/blog/essential-guide-writing-smart-goals
4. Warren Bennis, *Why Leaders Can't Lead: The Unconscious Conspiracy Continues* (San Francisco: Jossey Bass Publishers, 1989), 18.
5. Peter Drucker, *The Effective Executive: The Definitive Guide to Getting the Right Things Done* (New York: Collins Press, 1967; reprint ed. 2006), xii.
6. Ron Chernow, *Titan: The Life of John D. Rockefeller, Sr.* (New York: Vintage Books, 1998), 181.
7. William Manchester, *The Last Lion: Winston Spencer Churchill Alone 1932-1940.* (New York: Delta Publishing, 1988), 61

8. Lyle Dorsett, *A Passion for God: The Spiritual Journey of A.W. Tozer*(Chicago: Moody Press, 2008), 160.

9. White, Ellen G, *Patriarchs and Prophets* (Interamerican Division Publishing Association 2002),425.

NOTES